Ex Libris

St. Paul's Church

40 COLOR PLATES BY ERICH LESSING

57 ENGRAVINGS BY G. B. PIRANESI

TRANSLATED

BY ROLAND HILL

HERDER AND HERDER

ROME REMEMBERED

BY WERNER BERGENGRUEN

INTRODUCED BY

CLARE BOOTHE LUCE

1835

1968
HERDER AND HERDER NEW YORK
232 Madison Avenue, New York, N.Y. 10016

BURNS & OATES LTD.
25 Ashley Place, London S.W. 1

The illustrations in the text are reproductions of
engravings made by Giovanni Battista Piranesi 1720–1778
for his great work "Vedute di Roma" (from 1748).

Library of Congress Catalog Card Number: 68–57654
First published in West Germany © 1968 Herder KG
Printed in West Germany by Herder

INTRODUCTION

Not long ago, I received a postal card depicting the Colosseum. It came from a talented young friend who was writing a novel which called for some chapters with a foreign background.

What W. S. Gilbert in the nineteenth century called "the fascination frantic / For a ruin that's romantic" had naturally enough, led my young friend to Rome. A sensitive, even scholarly sort, his first encounter with the Eternal City must have moved him deeply. But he was no doubt aware that generations of writers before him had been defeated in their attempts to match their prose to the lofty and profound emotions their own first sights of Rome had aroused in them. He simply scorned the ancient challenge. He scrawled on the back of his card, "Man, like I mean Rome *zaps* everybody!"

Rome does indeed zap everybody – the philosopher, the historian, the archaeologist, the poet, and the artist, and even that least zappable character – the tourist.

In its totality, Rome is inexhaustible, incomprehensible, and indescribable. Lived there a man with the eye auf Michelangelo, the mind of Thomas Aquinas, the soul and spirit of Dante, the will power of Caesar, and the lifespan of Methuselah, he just might be able to grasp Rome, and – in a hundred tomes – describe it. Barring the advent of such a one, all other writers, painters, and photographers can produce no more than jottings, sketches, vignettes. These, however, are not to be despised. The smallest fragments of knowledge garnered about Rome are worth an encyclopedia about any other city. For Rome is comparable to no city – except itself, which is to say, its many *selves*.

This book, with its engrossing text and its fine illustrations and photographs is one of the more valuable modern fragments that I have come upon in recent years. I say this as one who has spent far more time reading about Rome and thinking about Rome than I did during the years when I lived there as U.S. Ambassador. At this point I must make a confession. While I was serving in Italy, I tried, very consciously, to shove Rome – historical Rome – to the back of my mind in order to keep Italy and America in the forefront of it. For I soon sensed that historical Rome can *zap* the diplomat harder than anybody!

Few can do a job well who do not believe in the urgency and importance of it. To be effective, the diplomat must believe that his successful pursuit of his country's foreign policies is important, however relatively, to the prestige, power, and preservation of his nation. Never was this truer than in the nuclear age. Today the United States and Soviet Russia, the two mightiest nations the world has ever seen, are more or less evenly matched. They are locked in an enormous struggle for ideological supremacy over the hearts and minds of mankind. The outcome of this battle into which all the nations have been drawn remains in the balance. Neither the Western diplomat nor the Iron Curtain diplomat can afford to let slip away even trivial diplomatic victories. Consequently, each is expected by his own government, and especially by his own countrymen, to pursue his mission in a spirit of ideologic zeal and passionate patriotism.

But of all the frames of mind required of any professional, this is, precisely, the hardest to maintain in the Eternal City.

The diplomat is history minded. His very profes-

sion is the making of history, at the cutting edge, where sovereign powers come into conflict in mutually abrasive situations. A knowledge of the history of his own country (generally he refers to it as "the proud history") and equally the history of the country in which he is serving, is essential to the diplomat. For he knows that when history repeats itself, it often does so as tragedy. He must know and study history in order to identify those situations which in the past have led to war, or the diminishment of his country's world position, in order not to let them be repeated.

To live in Rome is, inescapably, to think about history. The rub for the diplomat is that Rome forces him to think about such a long, long, long span of

Page 9

THE CAPITOLINE SHE-WOLF which, according to the legend, found and suckled the founders of Rome, Romulus and Remus, became the symbol of the Roman World Empire. The bronze statue in the Capitoline Museum is of Etruscan workmanship from the 6th/5th century B.C. Originally probably the totem of a Latin tribe, the she-wolf came to signify the divine origin of the Roman people.

Page 10

VIEW FROM THE VIA SISTINA to the obelisk on the top of the Spanish Steps leading to the church of Santa Trinità dei Monti. The obelisk, a Roman imitation of an Egyptian model, once decorated the Gardens of Sallust. Under Pius VI in 1789 it was erected in the Piazza.

Page 11

THE CLOISTER OF SAN PAOLO FUORI LE MURA is of Romanesque origin and was begun under the Benedictine abbot Pietro da Capua (1193–1208) and finished by 1214. The round arched arcades are supported by small twin-columns decorated with mosaics of varying design by the brothers Pietro and Jacopo Vassaletto.

Page 12

A SANCTUARY OF MITHRAS in the Lower church of San Clemente. It is evidence for the varied history of the early Christian community which used the residence of St Clement, the fourth successor of Peter, for their gatherings. It is believed that the Saint's house was confiscated in the year 303 by virtue of the Edict of Diocletian and awarded to the priests of Mithras for their cult introduced to Rome from the East. It was later restored to the Christians.

Page 13

THE STATUE OF CHRIST as the good shepherd, also in the Lower church of San Clemente, illustrates the type of the youthful beardless Christ which goes back to ancient models based on statues of Apollo.

Page 14

THE CHURCH OF SANTI QUATTRO CORONATI was erected in the 4th century and destroyed by the Normans in 1084; the present church was rebuilt on a smaller scale by Pope Paschal II in 1111 and restored in 1914. The pavement is cosmatesque work of the 13th century. The name of the four Saints to which the church was dedicated are traditionally held to be Severinus, Carpoforus, Victurinus and Severus, four Roman soldiers who were put to death because they refused to worship a statue of Aesculapius and thus suffered martyrdom; another possible link could be with five Pannonian sculptors who had refused to make a statue of Aesculapius.

history – indeed, three thousand years of it. And this is to think about the history of civilization itself. Rome is the magnificently illustrated history book of the Western world. The diplomat does not perhaps "read" that history book as clearly as the historian. But what he does read is profoundly significant to him – and painful. He can scarcely miss the point that Rome heavily features the decline and fall of "invincible" empires, the birth and death of many "proud and prosperous" nations, the evolution, merging, and disappearing of scores of cultures, ideologies, religions. The moss-covered tombs of magnificent emperors, the whited sepulchres of great kings, the crumble and ruins of princely palazzos, Caesar's forum and Mussolini's – what are they all but sermons in stones on a single theme: *sic transit gloria mundi*. The monuments are the message. Or, as my poetic friend might put it – POW****₊*!! to the pretensions of all "sovereign nations".

A very dispiriting message indeed, and one no ambassador, Western or Eastern, would care to cable back to his own government.

A Roman tour of duty would be easier for the diplomat who would like to believe that his own young, modern ideology is the final answer for a brave new world, if only Rome also taught some ideological or political lesson. Such as, that in the long view of history, cultures collapsed, or rulers lost their hold over the populace, or nations perished, because of some error or failure common to them all. Unhappily, Rome rather tends to teach the opposite. During the long reaches of its history, art, architecture, poetry, literature, and religion did flourish under occasional benign and peaceful rulers. But they also burgeoned under brutal war lords, and mad and murdering emperors. In Rome, which has witnessed approximately every form of government ever tried by man, the wages of wisdom and virtue, no less than those of folly and sin, seem to be failure and death. (Here I am nevertheless tempted to wonder what the Soviet Ambassador thinks of the seemingly sole exception, represented by St Peter's golden dome – the symbol of the oldest enduring *institution* in the world – the Church of Christ.)

It is no wonder that in such a city (whose other name is *Déjà vu*) the diplomat sometimes becomes sceptical, even cynical, about the value of his own relatively puny efforts to assure his country a durable place in history. "Sicklied o'er with the pale cast of thought" he is prone to do as the Romans too often do, and slip into a mood of easeful fatalism, which he then calls his "sense of history", or "philosophical outlook".

"Ma chère colleague", an Allied diplomat once chided me, when I sought his support on a diplomatic question affecting the welfare of Italy, "what can it possibly *matter,* a hundred years from today, at five o'clock in the afternoon, whether or not the Italians are granted this concession?"

He waved his hand towards the window, from which there was a view of an old Roman wall, glowing rosy and golden in the warm afternoon sun. "Let us enjoy the light on that old wall, while we can", he sighed. Later, he told me that he planned to retire in Rome when he had finished his mission. He did not know it, but he had already retired. He had retreated into Roman history. He had given over to the Roman shards and ruins with their melancholy reminder that

15

"all this, too, shall pass", including, one day, the "glory" of his own glorious country.

And yet – and yet, for many people, of whom I am glad to count myself one, "the grandeur that was Rome" – many Romes – has a message far more compelling than that "all the paths of glory lead but to the grave". Rome bade me to glory, not in power, nor wealth, nor even in God (who may be gloried in anywhere). It bade me glory in man himself, man the free-swinging pendulum between good and evil, with his enduring capacity to hope and love, suffer and have faith, man who is brutish, but never a monster, man who is the ruin of a god.

It is as the City of Man that I remember Rome.

CLARE BOOTHE LUCE
Former U.S. Ambassador to Italy

16

THE WALLS OF ROME

We are all familiar with the traditional division of ancient Rome in the seven hills on the left bank of the Tiber: Capitoline, Palatine, Aventine, Coelian, Esquiline, Viminal and Quirinal. However, in the sea of houses that is modern Rome the old design is by no means easily traced. The city began to expand early on towards other heights too, towards the Pincio, the Ianiculum and the Vatican. Eventually, the city extended towards the outlying heights of Monte Mario, Monti Parioli, Monte Verde to the south on the right bank of the river, then towards the hill of S. Paolo and even as far as Monte Sacro, where the plebeians went on that legendary exodus which, had it not been checked, might have changed the history of Europe. Some of the hills have several tops to which, somewhat arbitrarily a single collective name has been given. Roman legend required the ever sacred number seven, thus riding roughshod over the logic of the city's geography. What there can be no doubt about is that Rome originated from her hills.

Just as the Colosseum is regarded by popular opinion as the most important site of Christian martyrdom – actually this was Nero's circus situated in the present Vatican area – so tradition has located the origin of the city on the Capitol as the site most fully endowed with symbols of the ancient Roman State. But in fact, the first settlements were on the Palatine and on the Quirinal.

Rome's origins are lost in darkness. Contrary to tradition, it is a city that has grown, not one that was founded, as the Romans, worshippers that they were of human resolution and acts of the will liked to think.

The area was evidently most suitable. The hilly terrain with its steep slopes and ravines, surrounded by marshy lowlands, the many little streams promised security and easy defence. The river formed the frontier with Etruria. Its crossing could be controlled and the island in it facilitated the building of bridges.

The first settlers were shepherds and Rome was to become the city of the supreme Shepherd of Christendom. Latin shepherds settled on the Palatine, while others coming from the Sabine hills, made their homes on the Quirinal. Eventually both peoples merged. The transition from a pastoral to an agricultural community was probably the result of a lengthy development. The area expanded, Etruscan influence grew. It was probably under the Etruscans that Rome became a city; indeed, the very name may be of Etruscan origin. When the Etruscan kings were overthrown, the ruling class of Latin, Sabine and Etruscan elements founded the republic.

THE PALAZZO
DELLA CONSULTA
*at the Piazza del Quirinale was
built in 1734 by the Florentine
architect Ferdinando Fuga
(1699–1784).*

A female rustic spirit named Pales, whose festival on April 21st is regarded as the founding date (753) of the city, appears to have inspired the name of the Palatine. Her name, possibly connected with *palus,* swamp, is the root of our "palace", "paladine"; and all the Palais de danse throughout the world remind us of the effects of that epoch-making hill.

Modern research has certainly been right in eliminating from Roman history everything that is mere myth, and yet the traditional legends contain elements that have had a more powerful effect on man's life on earth than all the documented facts of history. In Rome we are on mythical ground. The tales of the ancient world, the legends of the early Christian era contain a whole treasury of truths, even though they may not accord with our kind of truth of superficial reality. It must not be forgotten that in that distant past the question concerning the literal truth in our

TRAJAN'S COLUMN,
decorated with a spiral frieze
illustrating the Dacian Campaigns,
was erected in 113 A.D. *Facing it*
the churches Santa Maria di Loreto
(1507) and Santissimo Nome
di Maria (1738).

sense was never asked, either regarding the traditions of history or of legends, or those of the veneration of relics so frequently connected with legends. An entirely different kind of truth was derived by the men of those times from myths and sagas which for them replaced the pragmatic record of history. Of one thing we may be sure: people in the past had no less intelligence than we have to know that the lock of hair of Mary the Mother of Jesus preserved in the church of Santa Costanza is not real in the uncouth sense in which the snippings of our hair on the floor of a barber's shop are real. But just as to ancient man the image suggested the godhead without his confusing both, so did, for example, Mary's comb preserved at Trier suggest her presence. In the same way the written, spoken word cannot make tangible for us what it refers to but is not identical with it. And it is in this way that we ought to approach also the traditions of early Roman history, indeed Rome herself which in all her impulses has always been both reality

19

and myth. The tough, sober sense of the Romans, coupled with their ability stubbornly to cling to what once they have made their own has ensured that neither of these two possibilities wholly excludes the other.

It is because of the traditional name of "Roma Quadrata" rather than because of the few preserved remains that we may infer the square design of the original city wall which probably corresponded to the shape of the Palatine. It is likely to have been a wall of modest proportions, with two gateways, such as we may remember from drawings in our school books. When it was completed – perhaps when it had only just been marked out on the ground – Remus is supposed to have jumped over it, evidently to ridicule what his twin brother Romolus, the architect, claimed as his achievement. In a fit of rage, Romolus slew Remus and exclaimed "Thus shall be the fate of anyone who dares to scale this wall". The long centuries of Roman history have borne out the truth of his words.

A fratricide thus stands at the beginning of Roman tradition, reminiscent of the profound story of Cain and Abel. Not much else is known of Remus. But we may be entitled to think that with this bloody deed an active passionate man rid himself of a wearisome and carping sceptic, unfit for action, and so paved the course of Roman history. This legend, too, reflects something of the primitive notion that if a building was to remain intact some live sacrifice had to be entombed within it. A similar idea recurs in the story of the Curtian Lake, a deep and dangerous chasm, which had opened in the Forum, into which a soldier, Marcus Curtius, leaped voluntarily, armed and on his horse. The chasm closed. The spot was regarded as sacred and can still be seen.

On arriving in a city, it is an old habit of mine first of all to visit the walls and, if possible, to walk round them from inside and out. Even though the walls may well have disappeared long ago, it is usually possible, with some experience and by observing the lay-out of the streets, to trace their outline; sometimes even the names of the streets may be a help. In this way I make myself familiar with the historical origin and growth of a city through visual experience rather than through oral or written information. Not being a driver but a leisurely pedestrian, I have not found this sort of discovery an easy system for Rome; anyway, it meant many and long walks. The Roman city walls have always had a significance different from those of other European cities. The proud Latin word *"urbs"* links with *"orbis"*, meaning something encircled or enclosed. The Romans tended, as the words indicate, not only to place them in opposition to one another, but in a certain sense, almost to equate them. Urbs, the city, that is, the city *par excellence,* was exclusively their own – Rome. They wished to suggest that compared with her not even Athens, Byzantium, or Ephesus appeared to them worthy of the civic dignity; they were places, *oppida, municipia, coloniae,* but Rome alone was the world.

Stone walls were the typical setting of the people of antiquity as they still are today of the Mediterranean races and Italy, is, of course, a country of cities. A wall is not just a protection against enemies; it also demarcates the area of human civilization against untamed nature outside, that seems ruled by sinister forces beyond the control of man.

20

THE PALAZZO BARBERINI,
one of the most imposing in Rome,
was begun by Carlo Maderna for
Urban VIII, continued by
Francesco Borromini and finished by
Gian Lorenzo Bernini in 1633.

Outside the city walls were the incalculable forces of the world of demons, a sinister link, as it seemed, to ancient men, with the Barbarian world. The wall was the symbol of human, urban civilization and therefore sacred and pleasing to the Gods. We shall never understand ancient man and his notion of life unless we remember the metaphysical no less than military significance of these protective walls. Even today, in southern countries, we find stone walls rather than the fences or hedges customary in northern countries. "Murus", is a primordial factor in the lives of the southern races; it is that which makes a city what it is.

After the coalescence of the settlements on Palatin,

Page 23

PORTA SAN SEBASTIANO, with its mighty towers erected in the 5th century by the Emperor Honorius and restored by the Byzantine General Bellisarius (500–565). Here is the beginning of the Via Appia, the Roman road of tombs.

Page 24

THE SERVIAN WALL dates back as far as the legendary beginnings of Rome. It was erected by Servius Tullius, last but one of the Roman kings of the Etruscan dynasty, before 500 B.C. Remains of this enormous construction are to be found near the Stazione Termini, Rome's central station.

Page 25

THE AURELIAN WALL, twelve miles long, which protected medieval Rome was built by the Soldier-Emperors Aurelianus and Probus from 271–276 A.D. Until the Baroque age this wall was repeatedly fortified as is shown by the coat of arms of the popes who were responsible for the repairs of particular sections.

Page 26

THE SISTINE CHAPEL IN THE VATICAN was built for Sixtus IV by Giovanni dei Dolci (1473–1481). The frescoes of the walls were decorated between 1481 and 1483 by Umbrian and Tuscan painters, on the left wall the Life of Moses, on the right wall the Life of Christ. The ceiling is entirely decorated with the famous frescoes begun by Michelangelo on May 10th 1508 and completed by him on October 31st 1510, showing the story of creation and the fall of man. Prophets and sibyls and scenes from the genealogy of Christ complete the enormous work. More than twenty years afterwards, commissioned by Pope Paul III, Michelangelo walled up two windows and destroyed three frescoes by Perugino, and painted the Last Judgement 1536–1541 on the wall over the altar, with altogether 391 figures on an area measuring 63×32 feet.

Page 27

THE PORTA ASINARIA with its large round towers was erected in the 15th century. In the background the roof top of the church of San Giovanni in Laterano.

Page 28

CASTEL SANT'ANGELO, built 135–139 A.D. as a mausoleum for the Emperor Hadrian. Having been used as a papal fortress in the Middle Ages, the building received its present form by Bernini (1660–1667). Bernini also designed the ten statues of angels on the Ponte Sant'Angelo. The name Castel Sant'Angelo is derived from an apparition of St Michael in 590 announcing to Pope Gregory the Great the end of the plague.

Quirinal, and Viminal, and the subsequent expansion of the urban area, Rome became, if we disregard partial fortifications such as that on the Capitoline Hill, an open city, to use a modern term. In the great invasion of the Gauls under Brennus the city was almost completely destroyed. A new wall was built, and was later ascribed to Servius Tullius, the sixth and last but one of the Roman kings. The number of the early rulers had of course to be the same as the sacred number of the hills.

The Servian Wall enclosed a considerable part of the city's original outline, completing the merging of the seven hills into one city. It followed the course of the Tiber only from the Aventine area to a point south of the Capitol. Outside this area there remained the Campo Marzio, the Martian Fields, between Capitol, Tiber and Pincio. This meadow land was at first used for martial displays. Then the great buildings of state and temples arose here, the Theatre of Pompey where Julius Caesar met his death on the Ides of March, the Flaminian Circus, the building of Agrippa, among them the Pantheon and the Mausoleum of Augustus. This area later became the centre of papal Rome. Underneath it and never to be uncovered lie the remains of the Rome of the Caesars.

The Servian fortification built out of stone and earth must have been quite formidable, about 90 feet wide and 45 feet in height. In some places the wall is still visible today: massive stones laid upon one another without mortar, with buttresses and trusses alternating. There are some impressive remnants near the main railway station in the courtyard of the customs office, with three palm trees rising above it; part of the west wall can be found in the middle of the picturesque Piazza Magnanapoli, also under palm trees. A third part, unearthed only in this century, lies in the modern surroundings at the junction of Via Salandra, Via Carducci and Via Piemonte. A Latin inscription tells us: "Walls once protected the city, now the city protects her walls." Another part of the wall, some 150 feet long, can be seen on the southern slope of the Aventine rising upwards. Whence it turned northeast up to the Porta Capena. The Via Appia, leading towards Capua, begins here. There are a few green trees between the Aventine, Palatin and Coelian on the spot still today as Porta Capena; but all that remains of this most famous of the old Roman gates are a few boulders in the grass. It was probably through this gate, then surrounded by the stalls of Jewish merchants, that St Paul entered Rome as a prisoner. This was the site of one of the three ancient Jewish settlements in Rome and very likely also of the first Roman followers of Christ.

On the Esquiline, too, not far from the north-eastern end of the Baths of Trajan we find a remnant of the Servian wall in the shape of scattered stones nesting against a famous ruin. It is a hall, small and intimate by Roman standards, with tiers rising as in an amphitheatre. There are still traces of Pompeian red on the walls, five alcoves with painted garden scenes like mock windows. It is a moving experience to note trifling details which have survived destruction, such as a figure pouring out water for a dog; the painted thin jet of water can still be seen after two thousand years. The building is known as the Auditorium of Maecenas. Man tends to link unknown with known factors and, rather than to leave things in obscurity, to connect them with famous names. That was the way of the Romans as of the learned humanists of the Renaissance. What they rediscovered, was immediately endowed with the great names of antiquity. A damp cave was thus discovered to be the grotto in which the wise King Numa Pompilius met the goddess Egerian who was said to aid him with her counsels by night. Some rubble in the Esquiline area, parts of the aqueduct built by Julius Ceasar, was ascribed to Marius. And the Servian Wall had a similar fate. It is the same with people who believe in the migration of souls; everyone wants to have been Alexander the Great, no-one contents himself with having been merely one of his numerous footmen or kitchen slaves. Scholars may object that the Gardens of Maecenas, situated as they were further North to the right and left of the Servian wall, could hardly have extended to the auditorium and that it is difficult to see it as a lecture room. And yet, why should we not delight in imagining that this was the place where, before a distinguished audience, Horace recited his poem, "Maecenas atavis edite regibus – Oh Maecenas, scion of proud ancestral line", acknowledging the applause of the public with a slight ironic bow. Why not leave it at that?

In the days of Horace, Maecenas and Augustus, Rome had long grown far beyond the Servian wall. But by this time no other protection was needed than that formed by the shields of her legions. Indeed, it was fortunate that Rome had enclosing walls. At the time of the civil wars, she was thus saved from sieges, assaults and destruction. It was only when she could no longer count on the support of her legions that new means of fortifying the city had to be found.

At a time of decline and danger, when in a single half century alone only one out of twenty six Roman Emperors died a natural death, Aurelius and Probus took five years, from 271 to 276, to build the formidable fortifications which can only be compared with the Great Wall of China. It was no coincidence that both emperors were also the architects of the famous limes stretching from the middle Danube up to the Taunus Mountains on the banks of the Rhine. The building of the Roman city walls indicates judgment rather than a helpless fear of the barbarians and their invasions. It seems that this gigantic undertaking was the expression of strength as yet unbroken, however much contested, of enduring Roman self-confidence, as well as of the continuing effect of Rome's civilizing mission. The Aurelian wall lasted beyond the Middle Ages. It did not save the city from being conquered several times, but without it Rome would not be standing today. The wall was joined on the right bank of the Tiber with the battlements built by Leo IV and IX and by Urban VII in the seventeenth century and for the first time parts of the right bank were joined with the city. In the nineteenth century struggle for the possession of Rome this wall played its part; it still stands today, seventeen centuries after the foundation, uniting the ancient with the medieval, even with the modern world in the truly Roman fashion of living continuity.

This wall is part of the basic Roman features, and as in ancient times, so even now, in some respects, it divides *urbs* and outside world. It is still the self same gates through which the traffic pours into and from the city. Some gates resemble medieval castles, others triumphal arches. Some seem to defy admittance, others to welcome the visitor in the grand and festive

30

PORTICO OF OCTAVIA,
*dating from 149 A.D., rebuilt
however by Augustus (23 B.C.),
who dedicated it to his sister Octavia,
and later by Septimius Severus and
Caracalla.*

manner. To the latter belongs specially the Porta del Popolo to the north of the city through which in the ages before the railway all those from beyond the Alps entered Rome, emperors and pilgrims, and among them Queen Christina of Sweden, in whose honour the gate was restored and embellished by Lorenzo Bernini. One hundred and thirty years later Goethe recorded passing through the gate on his first visit to Rome.

The third circle of walls has always been one of my

31

favourite Roman walks. I have gone along it at all times of the day, in the heat of noon, at dusk, by moonlight, and in all kinds of weather. I leave the city, as travellers did in ancient times, by the Porta Capena. I walk south-eastwards, along the wide avenue of trees and broken ancient columns. The road continues exactly in the line of the Circus Maximus between Aventine and Palatine. On the right are the ruins of the Baths of Caracalla, massive stumps of stone, and on the left the green south-western slope of the peaceful Monte Celio. I pass by the little early Christian church of SS Nereus and Achilleus reaching the narrow garden-lined street that leads to the Porta Latina and thus to the third wall circle. There are no shops, no bars, hardly any houses. Hidden in the grass, here and there, lie early Christian and ancient tombs such as those of the Scipio family who owned land in these parts. From behind a garden wall rises a pine tree thickly entwined with ivy and Virginia creeper that has grown beyond the parasitical ivy and hangs down from the branches in reddish golden streamers that sway in the light breeze. It is one of those chance glimpses one never forgets. Left, in front of the city gate and a little apart stands the fifth-century church of San Giovanni a Porta Latina, built on the spot where there was once a temple of Diana. I have always felt a mysterious attraction when in the church calendar I come to the entry, on May 6th "St John at the Latin Gate". The spot is secluded and quiet, an entrance hall supported by columns, to the left also flanked by two columns an ancient marble fountain and to the right the round three-sided brick structure from the midst of which rises a giant cedar tree. The sombre dark green of this tree seems to disseminate an aura of peace. The walls of the porch show traces of old frescoes and there are ancient grave-stones inserted here and there into the floor and lower walls. The interior of the little church overwhelms by its unostentatious purity. One seems to be transported back to the ages of the catacombs. The three naves are divided by ten ancient columns, five at each side. The three arched windows of the apse are made of thick-veined, brown-yellow alabaster through which light barely penetrates so that one can see little more than the outline of the crucifixion group, a twelfth-century fresco.

Returning to the street and looking towards the city, we have a lovely view of the dome of St Peter's through a narrow opening of trees. Some prefer this view to the famous one through the peep-hole in the garden door of the priory that belongs to the Knights of Malta, or even to the view of St Peter's from the Pincio. When seen from the Pincio, the dome seems to reach into the sky above all other buildings. But from the Via di Porta Latina it seems to be floating in the sky above the treetops, as though it was weightless, and no other man-made building is visible.

Simple as the church, is also the gate through which the road leads into the countryside of the province of Lazio. It was built from greyish stones between brick-towers that have fallen to ruins, topped by five turrets. The gate's opening is narrow. Immediately in front of it a small and graceful oratory marks a site honoured by tradition. This is San Giovanni in Oleo, and, according to the legend, it is where St John the Evangelist appeared unscathed after undergoing the torture of boiling oil. Walking through the gate we are confronted by the Aurelian wall on both sides.

The Roman suburbs are of more recent origin. When I first came to Rome nearly half a century ago, I still looked out from the parapet by the Lateran into the wide green and brown Campagna; today the view is hidden by huge blocks of flats. We may think of them as skyscrapers but they may equally well remind us of the many-storeyed tenement houses of ancient Rome. Some large fortunes were made by building speculators and their rack rents. If we turn right at the Latin Gate we shall even today get an impression of that tremendous desolation in which this area of the wall has been for centuries.

In the old cities of northern Europe houses were nearly always built against the inside of walls. These old cities are narrow, Rome is spacious. It has always enclosed many vacant plots of land, gardens, pastures,

vineyards, desolate sites used for dumping rubbish, and something of these conditions still prevails. In medieval Rome not much more than two thirds, in the worst times not even one third, of the area encircled by the wall was built upon. Hence along its more remote parts it is rare to find buildings higher than the wall. For the most part it pursues an uncluttered course encircled at the outside by wide quiet streets. On the inside there are gardens or waste areas. Looking up we see nothing but the towering, grey and reddish stonework here and there overgrown with greenery, and above it the silent sky. Between outer wall and road runs a spacious stretch of green. But no official gardener has ever tamed this wilderness with mowers or shears. Grass and weeds grow profusely undisturbed. Sometimes you see people gathering food for their goats and rabbits. Everywhere there are empty tins, old shoes, broken rusty pots and pans, pieces of old lavatories, everywhere burnt-out cinders, rubble and here and there stones which have tumbled from the wall. Take one with you if you feel like it, no one will stop you; at the most one of the locals passing by will smile at what may seem to him an act of folly. But for you such a profane relic may be like a lucky and protective charm, for after all, the little stone has had its share in protecting the heart of Western civilization from the Barbarian invaders.

In some places the wall reaches the height of big buildings in others it is only a few feet high; elsewhere again it presents a naked and bare appearance or it is covered by cascades of light green creepers or by darker growth like funebrial hangings. There are occasional small marble plaques bearing the crests of Popes who had been responsible for the repair of those parts of the wall. The little plaques seem modest and unpretentious compared to the pompous inscriptions with which the Roman architects used to record their achievements for posterity. It is as though there had been some awareness that the constructive achievements of individuals are but a small and humble service as against the magnitude of this almost timeless work of man. At short intervals square towers jut out, further westward there are bastion-like projections some of which, like grey mossy rocks seem magnificent retrogressions into nature. Nowhere has the attempt been made to support the wall's defensive might by moats. Such an undertaking would not have been worth the labour and costs. The water from the Tiber would not have sufficed in the hot season and outside the city the unprotected aqueducts in the open country might have been destroyed by the enemy.

The Porta Latina is followed by the Porta San Sebastiano, or Porta Appia as it was called in Roman days. For this is where the Via Appia leaves the city, that great road of tombs, silence and meditation. This highway leads right into the area of the catacombs and into the lonely seemingly infinite *Campagna;* it is, perhaps, the most history-laden road of the European continent, just as we may regard the Tiber as the most history-laden river. The Porta San Sebastiano with the dark stonework of the Arch of Drusus in front of it has the appearance of a mighty medieval bulwark. Approaching it one will notice a number of rusty iron hooks beneath the outer skirting; they supported the tapestries with which the gate was adorned for the entry of Emperor Charles V when he returned from his victories in Tunis. He was given a triumphal reception, for, by defeating the Muslim Corsairs, the

Emperor had also freed the Italian coast from a great menace. It seems as though the Romans were at that time inclined to forget all about the conquest and sack of Rome by the imperial mercenary army that had occurred only nine years earlier. These unimportant iron hooks are a nice example of the durability of trivialities. Long ago the sun set in Charles' world empire, the tapestries have long been eaten by the moth, but the hooks are still there. Beyond the Porta San Sebastiano, for a short stretch, the inward part of the wall is inaccessible because of villas, gardens and parks. The wall now surrounds the Aventine and its slopes as before it encircled the Coelian. Wide roads lead out into the countryside; there is much traffic, but one hardly meets any pedestrians. Looking back towards the city, we have in front of us the old circular church of Santo Stefano Rotondo, the two little steeples of the Lateran Basilica and, suddenly, from the road rising behind the Baths of Caracalla, the mountains towards the eastern, north-eastern and northern horizon.

In our walk along the wall we now approach the Porta San Paolo, also known by its old name of Porta Ostiensis on account of the Italian fashion of more recent decades to revive the ancient names, and because it leads towards the old Roman port of Ostia. The busy road towards the sea branches off near the Basilica of San Paolo, leaving solitude behind it and taking on suburban and urban character. The wall is pierced on a wide front, the gate lies in the very centre of the noisy street; it is not really a gate but a fortress on its own. I am reminded of a poem by the German poet Platen "The Pyramid of Cestius" which begins:

"Bleak memorial, huge and grave you gaze upon
Rubble only, gaze on gravemounts, on the hill of broken pieces over there,
And here on the Tiber turning away from Rome
And carrying with it the debris of civilization."

(Öder Denkstein, riesig und ernst beschaust du
Trümmer bloß, Grabhügel, den Scherbenberg dort,
hier die weltschuttführende, weg von Rom sich
wendende Tiber!)

I think that no description can conjure up more clearly, and with greater dignity and *Romanità* the spirit of this locality. For this is the very spot where the river begins to part from the city and where between the Pyramid of Cestius and the Monte Testaccio (the hill of broken pieces originally formed from the debris of *amphorae testae*) the tall cypresses of the Protestant Cemetery rise over the wall. The pyramid-shaped tomb which the Praetor Cestius had erected for himself a decade before the birth of Christ is built into the wall. Although the base is covered by the ground, it rises to a height of 121 feet. Its spotty grey turns whitish towards the top as though bleached by the sun. The wall is well preserved at this point, square turrets evenly forming part of it, many still with the old battlements. Now the wall approaches the river; buildings and railway sidings compel a detour. In the area of the former Tiber Harbour, a few steps south of the Ponte Dell'Industria, a last stretch of ruined wall reaches the yellow waters, and thence only a few stones can be traced a short way up along the river. If we turn left from the Porta Latina, going first northwards then towards the east, we shall have

THE BATHS OF CARACALLA
*begun by Septimius Severus in 206,
inaugurated by his son Antonius
Caracalla, are the most spectacular
ruins of the city of Rome.*

a sense of the old loneliness and grandiose desolation. The stones of the wall have crumbled away, bits of masonry cover the ground, most of the upper part is missing. There are few shops, hardly any cafés where we might rest from our walk by taking a *Campari soda* or *café nero* at the bar. Between wall and street there are small allotments, tennis courts, sports grounds, vast chaotic mounds of scrap iron and building materials; lorries are parked here and the decorated vans belonging to travelling fairs. The streets are scarcely paved; they are covered with rubble and any amount of dirt and litter as is the custom among the happy-go-lucky Southerners. Certain hollow parts of the inner wall are inhabited by the homeless; they have built themselves little hovels out of a few wooden boards, curtain rags, sheets of corrugated

iron and old wooden boxes. Similar wretched habitations can be seen near the Baths of Caracalla or opposite the Colosseum at the slope of the Temple of Claudius. Bits of washing are strewn to dry over the bushes, smoke rises from an improvised hearth and a heap of newly plucked chicken feathers suggests that today, at least, want is not as unbearable as it might be. There is much singing, children are crying, hens cackling, dogs barking. When the residents are away, a tethered mongrel guards the homes that cannot be locked.

The wall serves at this juncture to enclose the buildings of the Lateran. Above it rises the Lateran Palace and the church of St John Lateran which since the days of her founder, the Emperor Constantine, carries the proudest of all titles *"omnium urbis et orbis ecclesiarum mater et caput – Mother and Head of all the churches of the City and of the World"*. We pass to the Porta San Giovanni with the wide road leading to Frascati, Rocca di Papa, Genzano. The original edifice of the gate, the ancient Porta Asinaria flanked by two high circular towers, is blocked up and partly demolished. Beside it stands the ornamental gate of Gregory XIII from the sixteenth century, with three round-arched exits to each side. A few yards before the next city gate, the Porta Nolana, near the spot where the vast elliptic remains of the former Amphitheatrum Castrense have become part of the wall, where the monastic building of Santa Croce di Gerusalemme are visible behind it, we have, looking back, the most magnificent view of the majestic Lateran Basilica. The roof of the entrance hall with the cosmic spectacle of the crucifixion rises up like a vast stage above the city wall. Dominating everything else stands the dark cross with the figure of Christ in front, his hand raised in blessing, taking all upon himself in *urbem et orbem*. This view is absolutely breathtaking at dusk when the white statues glitter with the golden red light of the sinking sun, gradually losing colour and finally turning into black silhouettes against the golden sky. Behind the Porta Nolana, through which we would pass to reach Santa Croce in Gerusalemme, the wall of the Amphitheatre has preserved its strange brick-columned architecture.

Looking at Santa Croce may remind us that it was the ancient world, which erected the cross of Golgotha, and in which the Empress Helena brought that ignominious instrument of death back to this place as a triumphant symbol of life.

Now evening darkens the street, swifts shoot past through the cooling air like shadows. Enormous aqueducts seem to rise out of nowhere, cross the wall circle and merge with it.

At the Porta Maggiore, the Major Gate, the name of which indicates not only size but also the south-westerly direction towards the Basilica Santa Maria Maggiore, the ancient prevails over the medieval world. The castle from which the Colonna family controlled the road leading to their estates in the Sabine hills has disappeared. Arches built of big boulders guard the ornamented double entrance of what in pre-Aurelian times was part of the Claudian aqueduct. Almost against the gate is the curious tomb of the baker Marcus Virgilius Eurysaces and his wife Atinia, the circular openings of which represent the mouths of the baker's oven with a frieze above illustrating the stages of bread-making. Behind the Porta Maggiore the wall has been demolished to make room for the modern traffic, further on it serves, in well preserved state, with towers and parapets to fence in railway lines. Some of the houses have built against the wall for the densely populated area suffers no waste of space. Increasingly, houses, yards, gardens block the access to the inside of the wall. Here and there half way up we find something that looks like a little hanging garden. Tall aqueducts seem to butt against the wall.

The Porta di San Lorenzo has taken over the function of the ancient Porta Tiburtina which stands beside

PORTA MAGGIORE,
*built by the Emperor Claudius
in 52 A.D.; formed from two
enormous arches of the Claudian
aqueducts, and restored by Honorius
in 405 A.D.*

it, locked. Here begins the road to Tivoli, the Tibur of old. Most of the gates were at one time named after the town towards which they pointed; later these names were replaced by names of nearby churches. On the road to Tivoli stands the Basilica of San Lorenzo, the martyr; it is the third basilica beside San Paolo and San Sebastiano outside the city walls, "fuori le mura" and contains the tomb of Pius IX. It was partly destroyed in the last war and has been restored. Behind the Air Ministry and the Ministry of Foreign Trade the wall projects toward the east forming a rectangular area which was originally used for military purposes;

the Emperor Tiberius had it built for his praetorian guards. In the new university quarter the wall is quite straight, an almost even line without projections and recesses all along the tree-lined Viale del Policlinico. The height is the same height as that of the hospital buildings opposite. Occasionally one gets glimpses of the Sabine Mountains on the blue horizon. Where the wall curves round to the west there is a stretch that used to be covered by small votive tablets. This was the spot where a father and his four children during an air raid in March 1944 invoked the protection of the Virgin Mary and all escaped unharmed in spite of the hail of bombs. In gratitude for this rescue he donated a statue of the Blessed Virgin and the spot became a popular place of devotion. Flowers were planted, there were always lighted candles and people praying. It is a good example of the unsophisticated and natural manner in which even today sacred places can spring up in the very midst of modern life as they used to in the distant past. The Romans believe that the Virgin Mary protected their city also in troubled modern times and this is gratefully expressed in the inscriptions on many similar shrines.

It is difficult to say whether this city wall stirs the emotions more deeply where its own desolate appearance accords with the desolation of the surroundings or where, as in these north-eastern parts it faces the noisy bustle of the Roman day, imposing upon it a measure of its own silence. Naturally in the busy districts and between the gates, the wall is frequently cut through by streets, yet it manages, nevertheless to retain its identity.

The Porta Pia, designed by Michelangelo, was put up by Pius IV in 1561 and restored by Pius IX three centuries later in 1868. Shortly after its renovation this gate was the scene of the decisive battle for the possession of the city. The artillery of the young Italian kingdom battered a breach through which the Italian forces penetrated into the papal city vacated already by the French occupation forces. This was the end of the Papal States, Rome became the capital of a united Italy and the Pope the "Prisoner of the Vatican". Not until the signing of the treaty in the great hall of the Lateran Palace, sixty years later, was this most unhistorical and unnatural of Roman developments brought to an end. The Porta Pia is a decorative group of buildings rather than a mere fortified city entrance. The slender steeple-like top of the inner gate can be seen from far. Its high tower carries a coloured statue of Our Lady, beloved by the Romans, but of no artistic merit. She is turned towards the north-east welcoming the visitor into the city. A few steps away is the famous 'breccia' (breach) with a marble monument and a column that commemorates September 28th, 1870, a dignified and tasteful memorial. The brash spirit of Italian nationalism expressed itself in architectural terms only later. From Porta Pia the busy Via Venti Settembre leads towards the city centre and to the Quirinal Palace once the summer residence of the popes, then from 1870 to 1946 the residence of the kings of Italy, and now occupied by the President of the Italian Republic. Into the open Square of the Quirinale, which Goethe praised as "at the same time individualistic, irregular, grandiose and delightful", the spaciousness of nature seems to enter, just as the two colossal statues of Castor and Pollux holding their rearing steeds by the reins, suggest the mastery of space. Stately dignity seems at home here.

PIAZZA DEL QUIRINALE,
*flanked by the Quirinal and the
Palazzo della Consulta, residence
today of the President of the Italian
Republic. In the foreground the two
colossal groups (18 ft high) of the
Dioscuri Castor and Pollux,
Roman replicas, executed under the
Empire, of Greek originals of the
end of the 5th century B.C.*

Behind the Porta Pia the wall turns west and encloses that modern, secular area of the city which foreign visitors and diplomats choose as their residence. Here were once the gardens of the historian Sallust in the grounds where the large villa Ludovisi stood, some 360,00 square yards in area. All fell victim to the growing need for space, but also to the building speculators of the nineteenth century. At the foot of the ivy-covered wall, against the inside of which four and five-storeyed apartment houses have been built, lies a tomb of the Scipios.

The Porta Salaria, the Salt gate, through which Alaric the Goth entered Rome in 410 A.D. was taken down shortly before the first world war. In the days

41

VILLA ALBANI,
*nowadays called Torlonia after a
later owner, built about 1760 by
Carlo Marchionne for Cardinal
Alessandro Albani, who formed
there a valuable collection of antique
sculpture under the supervision of the
German archaeologist Johann
Winckelmann (1717–1768).*

when salt was produced at the sea shore it was carried along this road into the Sabine countryside. For in the beginning Rome was also, of course, a trading centre which she ceased to be only much later. For many centuries she lacked a middle class with artisan efficiency and was dominated by the five estates, clergy, the urban aristocracy, foreign visitors, servants and beggars. Even today, Rome has little significance as a commercial or industrial city compared to the number of her inhabitants. Rome is a city of officials, with less of luxury and night life than in rich and economically prosperous Milan, where prices and wages are also considerably higher than in Rome. Today the Via Salaria leads towards the Villa Albani, nowadays Torlonia, and its valuable collection of antique sculpture formed under the supervision of Winckelmann, a friend

*Veduta della Villa dell' Em̃o Sig.r Card.
Alesandro Albani fuori di Porta Salaria*

of Cardinal Alessandro Albani. It leads to the Villa Savoia, a former residence of the royal family, to the catacombs of Priscilla, and eventually to the site of the battlefield on the Allia where the Roman army was defeated by the Gauls three and a half centuries before Ceasar avenged it in his campaign in Transalpine Gaul. After that disastrous defeat Rome lay open to the pillaging and arson of the invaders from Gaul.

Behind the circular towers of the Porta Pinciana is the wide green area of the Villa Borghese, a spacious park and riding ground. In front is the road crowded by cars but without pedestrians. The walls which surround the Pincio merge into the huge supporting walls of the cliff-like slopes. Behind, high above, lies the Villa Medici, one of the marvels of Roman landscape gardening, with its severe symmetrical lines reminiscent of the Renaissance, with long, sombre paths lined by dark tall hedges. Nothing is left that could conceivably resemble meadows or woods; nature has been completely subjected to man and his notions of beautiful and noble living.

The wall circle gradually slopes down to the Porta del Popolo which replaced the old Porta Flaminia four centuries ago. Michelangelo is said to have designed it but it makes a hybrid impression. The wall which formally ended at the Tiber now extends a little way beyond this northern Gate, then disappears in the maze of modern roads.

The Aurelian Wall is roughly ten miles in length, about ten feet in width, the average height, varying though it is in places, is about fifty feet. In Rome's early days there were sixteen gates, two of them on the right bank. Today there must be close on two dozen, depending on which exists and entries are counted.

The towers of which there are many hundreds no longer dominate the scene as they once did. But this is not only true of the wall area. According to an old tradition, Imperial Rome resembled a dense grove of columns and statues. In the Middle Ages it was a forest of towers. Taking into account the towers on the walls, there are said to have been well-nigh a thousand. Each patrician family had its own tower, often erected over some ancient monument or built of its remains. They had a defensive purpose but also served as social prestige. This wealth of towers may have given medieval Rome the sort of appearance which the Tuscan town of San Gimignano has preserved up to the present day if on a somewhat smaller scale. Today there are barely two dozen old towers left in Rome, if we exclude those on the city wall and the many church Campanili. Most impressive among these towers is perhaps the formidable Torre delle Milizie, popularly known also as the Tower of Nero, for it was from this point that the Emperor is believed to have watched the burning of the city which he had ordered. The tower stands at a point half way up the Quirinal hill on the Piazza Magnanapoli, not far from the remains of the Servian Wall. At the nearby Forum of Trajan and the Markets belonging to it, the two storeys of shops are so well preserved that they could easily accomodate present day barbers, bakers and goldsmiths, too. Another of these patrician towers worth mentioning is the Torre dei Conti, a massive red brick structure which, in the Middle Ages, when people were fond of legendary exaggeration, was regarded as the most impregnable tower in the world. The whole area between Esquiline, Viminal and Capitol is really the region of towers, including the squat tower of the Palazzo Venezia. Some of these towers were later absorbed by other buildings. Thus one of them, formerly a maternal inheritance from Cesare and Lucrezia Borgia, became the church tower of San Francesco di Paola. It dominates the north-west corner of the quiet square outside San Pietro in Vincoli. In the morning the giant shadow of a vast palm tree swaying in the wind performs a fantastic dance upon its wall. Even more rare than such towers are the ordinary houses of medieval Rome, especially those which have preserved their own characteristics and have not been merged with the buildings of subsequent centuries. Nevertheless we can discover their traces even today.

The city on the right bank of the Tiber, the different parts of which grew into a single entity only in modern times, reflects this historical development also in the surrounding wall. To the Aurelian fortifications was added, though as yet not linked with them, the Leonine wall built in the ninth century by Pope Leo IV which surrounded the Vatican and the neighbouring quarter, the Borgo, to provide protection against the predatory raids of the Saracens. After the return of the Popes from their exile in Avignon, again at the time of the Renaissance, and under Urban VIII, the powerful Pope of the Baroque age, the wall was extended and reinforced. It begins in the south, at the former river harbour beneath the Aventine, a rather dull area. Very different from the wall on the left bank it suggests the classical style of Baroque fortifications. There are no towers, as they would anyhow merely have provided targets for the enemy's artillery fire, but instead of these there are flanking buttresses jutting out at acute angles and often with oblique escarpments. The wall

ascends to the top of the hill affording some wonderful views. At the outside it is accompanied by the restrained elegance of an expensive residential area. Towards the inside there are gardens, the most beautiful of which are those of the Villa Sciarra. The park was once famed for its innumerable peacocks, but they disappeared into the kitchens of the neighbourhood during the war and in the years of famine afterwards. From this point too, looking over the wall towards the sky, we sense that infinite solitude emanating from all Roman buildings.

On top of the Gianicolo, the old Janiculum hill, stands the Porta San Pancrazio. It was the scene of bitter fighting on a summer day more than a hundred years ago, when the French troops, sent to protect the Papal Government, fought their way into the rebellious city. Today this quarter lies peaceful and green in the sunlight. Beyond the Gate, is the vast Villa Doria Pamphili, perhaps the most beautiful of all patrician houses in Rome since the destruction of the Villa Ludovisi. Beyond it is the open country side and there is something of country air about the narrow road that leads to the red brick wall of the Carmelite church of San Pancrazio built over the catacombs. In spite of its Baroque embellishments the church has all the warmth and simplicity of the early Christian era. There is an inscription which tells that Pope Pius XII was christened in the baptismal font which was brought here later from the Church of SS Celso e Giuliano where the ceremony had taken place. The wall runs due north at this point linking up at the Porta San Pancrazio, formally the Porta Aurelia, with a stretch of wall of older origin which protected the outlying district of Trastevere, the old Transtiberium. The wall continues

VILLA DORIA PAMPHILI,
designed about 1650 by Alessandro
Algardi, the largest villa in all
Rome with a beautiful park area –
5.5 m. round its outskirts.

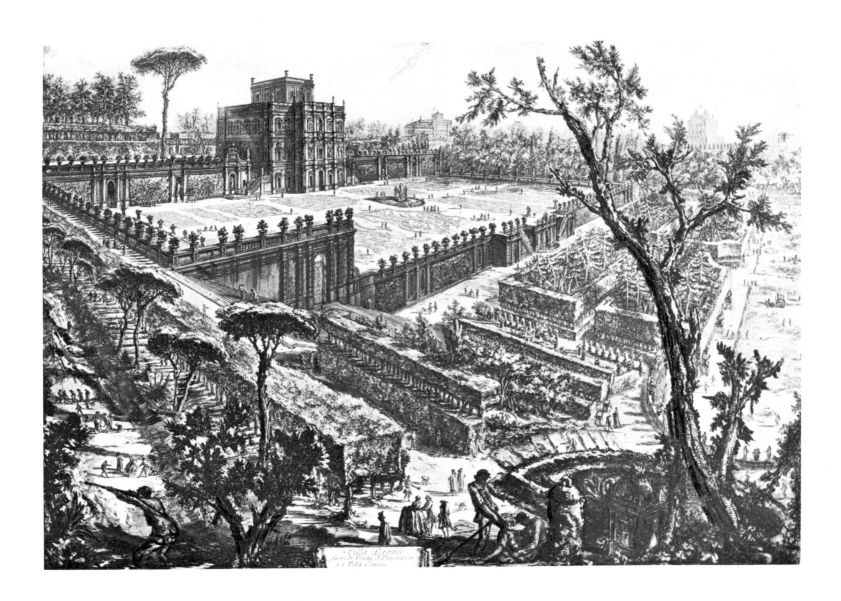

northwards almost in a straight line; outside, beneath the parts that support the slopes of the Gianicolo, there is open farming country towards the west, the old Etruria; towards the east, the view takes in the whole of Rome.

The road now descends towards the Vatican city, past the Monastery of Sant'Onofrio where the poet Tasso died and lies buried. Eventually, beneath the towering Collegio Urbano, the wall meets the colonnades of St Peter's. This is where, strictly speaking, the Vatican wall begins. Behind St Peter's the wall runs uphill and, although the left side of the street is bordered by houses, silence dominates. The masts of the Vatican radio station rise high above the wall like fretwork against the sky. Each one is surmounted by a cross, an effective illustration of the inscription on the Collegio Urbano *"Euntes docete omnes gentes* – Go and teach all nations". Behind the wall the tree tops of the Vatican gardens can be seen from the road. A few tall palm trees with fan-like branches are silhouetted against the sky. One senses a mysterious separation. Even the Dome of St Peter's is no longer visible. Hardly any other buildings can be seen – wall, green, sky, nothing else. Not until one approaches the Vatican Museum are there buildings once again, and indeed, the turmoil of the city.

There is something inexhaustible about Rome, not least reflected in the museums and collections. Collecting and assembling works of art has been a Roman tradition from the earliest days. Anyone who cannot spare a month or even years for special studies of Roman art history will have to make up his mind very soon what he should concentrate on. He has the choice between a superficial, even careless general view of the whole, of which his memory will retain no more than a part, and a painful but prudent limited selection. It is hard to admit that we as individuals are unable to make our own all that we regard as desirable or even feel to be indispensible. We must be selective, that is, learn to renounce and to do without. A few leaves from a forest of trees is all that we may gather in a course of a lifetime. Fortunate is he who takes them from plants which express something of the essence and basic universality of all vegetation.

So each one has to "do" Rome according to his own inclination. One's experience will be enriched in any case, be it merely by the fact of having "seen" or perhaps by some hazy though pleasant memories. What will remain in everybody's memory will probably be some breathtaking view from the windows of the Vatican on its courtyard gardens or buildings, Bramante's delightfully airy winding stairs, the Borgia apartments, inhabited by Alexander VI which seem to make tangible a great historical era, or the Gallery of Maps where the visitor walks all but 400 feet along maps of the Italian peninsula painted on the walls and dating back to an age when maps were not an exact graphic aid, but part of the picture of creation. The rooms seem vast, the horded treasures innumerable and immeasurable. Wandering through these rooms, is like wandering in a dream. The four large rooms of Raphael, the work of twelve years, are unforgettable. Even in their decayed state – the long gallery built by Bramante was roofed in only in the 19th century – the Logge of Raphael show a wealth of sumptuous ornamentation unique in the world. In the Sistine Chapel one may recollect Goethe's impression "Without having seen the Sistine Chapel we shall have no idea of man's capability. We hear and read of many great and good men, but here everything is above and before us, wholly alive". Nobody is likely to forget having stood in front of the famous Laocoon group or of the Apoxyomenos in the Cortile del Belvedere, that he looked on the Otricoli Zeus, the Belvedere Apollo or the Apollo killing lizards. The bust of Caesar will remain in the mind's eye, or some marvellous piece of ancient animal sculpture, or the famous Torso which Michelangelo admired and studied time and again. We may recall the two gods of the Mithraic cult, their lion zodiac on their vestments. There are the twin red porphyry coffins belonging to the Empress St Helena and her grand-daughters Constantia and Helena. The

46

Empress' sarcophagus is adorned with reliefs depicting the victories of her son, that of her grand-children with vine, ram and peacocks, the symbols of the early Christian era. To this list of memorable sights we may add the famous symbolic painting, the "Aldobrandini Nuptials", a masterpiece of ancient art, and the two pictures opposite, "Processions of children" and an ancient sacrifice offered by little children; these paintings were discovered at Ostia.

Of the tapestries linked with Raphael's name which on solemn occasions were used to cover the walls in the Sistine Chapel below the frescoes, perhaps the most impressive is the scene depicting Peter's miraculous catch of fish. There is the marvellous head of the lame man healed by Peter, next to it the scene at Emmaus or the tapestry showing the risen Christ, disguised as a gardener, appearing to Mary Magdalen. In the famous "Victory of Constantine over Maxentius" at the Pons Milvius we may perhaps remember among its innumerable details, the youth on horse back in the centre opposite Constantine, and Maxentius being carried off by the current of the Tiber. Who can forget Raphael's Madonna di Foligno, or his representation of the three cardinal virtues in which he denied himself almost any use of colour. Our list is likely to grow endless – with Leonardo da Vinci's unfinished

Jerome, with the sleeping young soldier in Perugino's Resurrection who is thought to be the young Raphael, and with those musician angels of Melozzo da Forli that used to be in the apse of the church of Santi Apostoli. A selection such as this ought to last a man a lifetime. We may add to it from pieces in the Capitoline Museum, the Baths of Diocletian or from the Roman collections of paintings. The beauty of it is that we can thus form a personal and private gallery, open at all times, in our own hearts.

Leaving the Vatican Museum we may follow the wall for a little way, but soon it disappears in the maze of buildings that are the product of fifteen centuries of changing needs and fortunes. The papal wall, built in the late Middle Ages, leads hence eastwards, crowned with battlements, frequently pierced by gate-like openings, finally rising to a considerable height. The fortifications to the north of the Vatican, built by Urban VIII have disappeared and in their place extends the modern district of Prati. The old East-West wall, however, still links the Vatican with the bulwark dominating the Tiber, the Castel Sant' Angelo. It is the only place of the Roman defences where use has been made of a moat. Here, at the old Mausoleum of Hadrian, our walk around the wall comes to an end; we have encompassed much more than a city.

THE WATERS OF ROME

Rome has many links with water, both as a natural element and as an object or ingredient of religious devotion. Nobody enjoying the wines of the Castelli Romani ought to forget the healthy, refreshing Roman water which Pius VI, for example, used to carry with him in large barrel-carts when crossing the Alps. Water also had a decisive impact on the history of the city. Alaric's Goths who conquered and sacked Rome in 410 damaged a large part of the old aqueduct and later Barbarian invaders under Witiges and Totila completed the work of destruction so that the densely populated hillside became uninhabitable. Urban life transferred to the lowland by the Tiber and the new city, papal Rome, arose on the Campus Martius.

The Tiber flows leisurely, as befits a river of such historical importance. In places it seems almost motionless. One can hardly believe that it is sometimes capable of working itself into fits of fury such as when its waters reached as high as the walls of the Church of Santa Maria sopra Minerva where the marks can still be seen.

The first contact the Tiber makes with the city is at the Ponte Molle or Ponte Milvio as it is known again today. There have been many similar evocations recently of the old names: Girgenti in Sicily, the ancient Agrigentum became Agrigento, the customary

Coliseo was restyled Colosseo, a name which only two centuries ago no Roman would have understood. Anyway one has to be thankful that the familiar, if corrupt Campidoglio has not yet been replaced by something like Capitolio. The Ponte Milvio, where the Via Flaminia approaches the city, north of the Porta del Popolo, is historically significant, for it was through his victory at the Milvian Bridge that Constantine established his sway and secured the future for Christianity. Not far from this bridge, in 1867, the Roman volunteers were defeated in Garibaldi's premature bid for the city. A short distance up-stream an enclosure of Baroque design marks the spring known as Acqua Acetosa, a mineral water, very pleasant if slightly sour to taste, which is supposed to contain calcium that has passed through the brownish-red volcanic pozzolane stone characteristic of Rome. A verse over the spout in somewhat pompous Latin praises the quality of the water and enumerates all the human organs that will benefit from it. By the way, even Tiber water was used for health purposes since it is said to contain a minimal proportion of sulphur. This unsavoury custom is supposed to persist even today. The Ponte Milvio was the terminus for the mail coaches from the north where travellers were received or left the city. On the bridge there is a statue of St John

PONTE MILVIO,
popularly also called Ponte Molle,
rebuilt in the 2nd century B.C. *made*
famous by the battle in which
Constantine defeated his rival
Maxentius in 312.

Nepomucen, patron of Bohemia, hardly otherwise known in Rome. It is nice to think that this patron saint of bridges was put here to welcome visitors arriving from his own parts of central Europe.

Including the Ponte Milvio, there are today 18 bridges over the Tiber. During the Middle Ages there were three, in the times of the Empires there were eight. At low tide the remains of Nero's bridge can be seen and below the ruins of the Emilian Bridge which was repaired again and again for almost eighteen centuries till it finally collapsed at the end of the sixteenth. The most magnificent bridge of all is the Ponte Sant'Angelo, the Pons Aelius of the Emperor Hadrian, leading to the Castel Sant'Angelo. Bernini and his pupils executed the ten giant angels bearing the instruments of torture of the crucifixion. Their

Baroque exuberance is in marked contrast to the severe and stern renaissance statues of Peter and Paul on the other side of the bridge. In times when freedom of speech was suppressed the Romans used to conduct discussions by way of verses pinned to the figures of the apostles. There was an even more famous, sometimes both illegal and satirical expression of public opinion, a written dialogue between the two ancient statues of Marforio and Pasquino; hence our "pasquinade" meaning lampoon or satire. Approximately at the same level as Saint Peter's there is a minute island in the river without a name of its own. I like looking at it. It sprawls like a dead *dachshund* with a few odd remains sticking out of the lifeless coating of grass.

More pleasant is another larger island situated further south between the old ghetto quarter and the Trastevere linked with the two banks by very old narrow bridges. The eastern bridge is called the Ponte dei Quattro Capi, the bridge of the four heads, after the two quadrangular ancient hermae to the right and left of the stone parapet. Nobody knows by what accident these ancient pillars, which used to be placed at street corners, came to be set up here. The island consists of two groups of tall buildings forming an intricate pattern and separated by a road linking the two bridges. It was once a sanctuary of Aesculapius, the god of medicine, and still contains two hospitals, one of them a Jewish hospital, for the ghetto is nearby, the other tended by the brothers of St John of God known as the Fatebenefratelli. On the site of the temple of Aesculapius we now find the church of San Bartolomeo built in the tenth century by Otto III who loved Rome and wooed the city like no other emperor. He dedicated it to the memory of his friend,

the martyred St Adelbert, Bishop of Prague and apostle of the Slavs. Since time immemorial there has been some connection between the island and the image of a ship. According to legend one of the sacred temple snakes kept at Epidauros was brought to Rome to provide an antidote against a deadly plague; when the ship arrived the snake slid overboard into the river and swam to the island. Later, when the stone embankment was erected, the island was given its final barque-like shape, a tall obelisk which has now gone, serving as its mast. Still, the campanile of San Bartolomeo can fulfil this role today. The resemblance to a ship is most noticeable at the southern end where a snake relief is preserved as a figurehead.

No other ships sail on the Tiber today. The once lively river traffic has gone and with it the harbour and also the wharf at the Ripetta so delightfully depicted in old engravings. Many charming old sights were destroyed when the embankment was built up and modernized.

Until the end of the fourth century B.C. the water supply of Rome depended on the Tiber as well as on the springs within the city and even at that time the supply was insufficient to meet the demands of the Romans with their increasing passion for baths and aquatic displays of every sort. Thus came about the great epoque of aqueducts which lasted three and a half centuries and was revived in the late Renaissance. Eleven aqueducts were built each more perfect than its predecessor in engineering skill, bringing the water by rows of arcades from the hills, rivers, lakes over distances of up to sixty miles. Some are still in operation today, the remains of others are a familiar feature of the city and the Roman Campagna. Added to the ancient aqueducts were earlier on the Cloaca Maxima

THE LITTLE TIBER
HARBOUR,
*called Ripetta, beneath the church
of San Girolamo degli Schiavoni
near Ponte Cavour.*

for the drainage of the swampy grounds of the Forum; these sewers are still functioning today. Their origin the old shrine of Venus Cloaca is recognizable; half way in their course leading to the Tiber they rise over ground, mercifully only for a few yards, but diffusing a horrible smell. Proudly an old woman used to show the site explaining that according to custom every inhabitant along the drainage line threw his refuse straight into it, and the patient pipeline responded with frequent stubborn blockages.

The numerous Roman *Terme* were not mere bathing places but at the same time, places of entertainment, sport, reading, indeed of social life in general, a luxury not just of the rich, but of the populace. The Roman politician like many politicians today had to play to the gallery to gain popularity and to canvass votes. He

THE CLOACA MAXIMA,
*the main sewer of ancient Rome,
flows into the river below the Tiber
island.*

achieved these ends by going one better than his predecessor or rival, by building baths, race courses, places of amusement and at the same time catering for spectacles, by distributing food and money. A man who could not afford this out of his own substance entered the service of the state and, for instance, as the exploiting procurator of some rich province made his own fortune. Many public buildings are intimately linked with the memory of evils that caused the degeneration, dissipation and final break-down of the strength of Rome.

The highly sophisticated life in the Roman baths details of which are most clearly expressed by the Terme di Caracalla and Diocleziano could only of

BATHS OF DIOCLETIAN,
the largest in ancient Rome,
inaugurated in 305/306 A.D. could
accommodate 3000 people.

course develop in a southern climate. There life is lived very much in the open because of the climate; craftsmen too, their jobs permitting, work in the street or in any open place. Houses are merely used for sleeping in. This way of life explains also the modest part played by books as compared with newspapers. A book seems to shun life in public and to presuppose the privacy of a home. Newspaper, however, are intended to be read and discussed in public, in streets or cafés. That was the kind of social intercourse that flourished in covered promenades and arcades, for instance in the double arcade of the Galleria Colonna or in that round building, based on the original design, where the Via Nazionale ends in the square in front of the Baths of Diocletian, with its many shops, bars and such like. It is also reflected in the popularity of the so-called "Alberghi Diurni" where one can have a bath, a massage, a hair-cut, buy newspapers, have

one's shoes polished, shirts washed and clothes quickly cleaned and pressed. These are living memories of the Roman tradition of the public bath.

The Terme di Caracalla are now a large heap of ruins covered with weeds. All the magic of the remains of ancient Rome, embraced by the great life-giving force of the earth, is at home here. Archeological research has explored and explained the function of each item, but actually seeing these ruins may make a yet greater impact. Some parts of the embellishments, especially the beautiful mosaic floors have remained. This is also where the two fountains stood that nowadays grace the Piazza Farnese. The Lateran Museum preserves portraits, larger than life, of champion athletes and gladiators found in the Terme di Caracalla; terrifying the violence of the muscles, those degenerate fore-

heads, the vacuous expression of their faces. The Terme di Diocleziano was the most extensive establishment, built according to tradition, by Christian prisoners. A large part of the building survived the Middle Ages. Under the direction of Michelangelo, almost ninety at the time, the Carthusian Monastery was constructed out of the ruins; it is famous for the large cloister disproportionate though it seems, and even better known because of its church, Santa Maria degli Angeli. It has no facade, nothing is visible from the outside save a brick-front of ruins. But on entering we are overwhelmed by sublime brightness. Light streams in from all sides. Something of the majesty of vast Roman rooms seems to be preserved, blended with the festive, joyful and measured harmony of the Renaissance.

Yet another church has been built from the ruins of the Diocletian Baths. The circular interior of the church of San Bernardo looks its best perhaps at dusk, when greyish light begins to spread below while bright light continues to percolate from above. It seems as though the light gradually fades through the cupola lingering there until it finally disappears. In one of the side chapels there is the marble tomb of the German painter Johann Friedrich Overbeck who in 1810, founded the Pre-Raphaelite brotherhood known as the Nazarenes, not a great painter, but an intensely idealistic artist. The old man's face is suffused with youthful peace, his recumbent body is clothed in the long fur-lined coat familiar from his portrait. There is a good deal in Rome to remind one of Overbeck and his Nazarene friends, Veit, Führich, Schnorr, and Cornelius. The group had its headquarters at the Monastery of Sant'Isidoro, south of Monte Pincio. The Casino Massimi in the Lateran area was decorated

by them with frescoes modelled on Dante, Ariosto and Tasso, and their works can also be seen at the Casa Bartholdy at the corner in front of Santa Trinità dei Monti which has long had artistic associations. The house was built by the painter and academician Zuccaro towards the end of the sixteenth century and for the last decades it has been the home of the Biblioteca Hertziana, a German research centre for art Historians. Incidentally the house is also the setting of Gabriele D'Annunzio's famous novel "Il Piacere".

The building and adorning of fountains is an old Roman tradition. In Imperial Rome there were said to be 1,352 public fountains. Scarcely any of these have remained intact, but many of the carvings have been preserved such as the magnificent animal heads that now surround the fountain in the courtyard of the Terme di Diocleziano. Innumerable designs from the ancient fountains, no less than the themes taken from the frescoes of the ancient bathing halls, have influenced later Roman and European artistic tradition. All those fish depicted in couples with their tails entwined, jolly little sea-horses snuggling up against the cheeks of the water-spouting deity, the courtiers of Neptune with their lower half covered in green moss after years and years under water, chubby-faced demi-gods of the sea blowing on conches. From their wind instruments blows not only water but, appropriately, also a sweet enchanting sound of the watery splash and tinkle. It is well expressed by the inscription "*Murmure suo fons canit vitae laudem* – by its murmuring the fountain sings the praise of life". These words are inscribed on one of the fountains of the Villa Borghese where the water spouts from the mouth of hares, with a nymph and a satyr with goat's legs swinging a baby faun between them. All the fountains of Rome seem to reverberate that Latin line.

If Rome is the city of fountains it differs in that respect from other cities and towns with fountains, as for instance in Switzerland, where they are largely commemorative or purely decorative. Roman fountains have specific and practical purposes. People drink from them, refresh their hands and faces, animals are watered, pots and pans are rinsed and the *fiaschi*, those indispensable belly-shaped, straw-clad Italian wine bottles. Many wives and servants still fetch drinking water, for the Roman tap water, excellent though it is, does not satisfy their fastidious taste. Grubby children's faces and other extremities are cleaned at the fountains and in the remote quarters of the city girls and women can still be seen doing the weekly washing.

The decorative motives of the Roman fountains show no great variety. Symbols of marine life are repeated over and over again, but often with original ideas; surprising and ever new are the effects of the particular local setting.

The great creator of Roman fountains was Lorenzo Bernini and the design of the most spectacular of all, the Fontana di Trevi, is also ascribed to his design. This is no mere fountain, but a palatial monument, the royal residence of the god of the sea. It forms one facade of the Palazzo Poli, which anyhow seems to exist solely for its benefit. There the artist has forgone all the usual sea animals and shells and other decorative elements. High up and in front of a columned recess stands triumphant Neptune and the folds of his robe merge with the stony waves support him. Below are the two winged water horses with their god-like companions, an imaginative variation on the horse and tamer-theme. One can have the impression from the triangular form of this group that it represents a chariot driven by Neptune, but in keeping with the water element everything appears so fluid that the artist's vision is not really susceptible of a fixed and concrete form. The water spurts out abundantly from the surrounding rocks, not from the mouth of animals, as though the Fontana di Trevi were a natural construction. Water is treated in its elemental character, the grey rough rocks have priority over sculptured marble.

The effect of a facade is also communicated by the Fontana Paolina (Acqua Paola) behind which one is tempted to imagine a whole suite of water chambers. This fountain served as a worthy reception for the five water pipes of Trajan's aqueduct on their arrival in Rome. Granite columns were taken from the portico of the former church of Saint Peter, marble from the Temple of Minerva at the Forum of Nerva, and with arches, pillars, columns, form the structure. There is less ornamentation except for the heraldic emblems which custom required. This fountain is prominently situated, below the porta San Pancrazio, high above Trastevere. One has a remarkable view of Rome, even if less extensive, than from other points on the right bank of the river. Opposite the Acqua Paola is the Spanish Embassy, the Academy of Arts and the church of the Monastery of San Pietro in Montorio. Under the steps of the high altar lies the body of Beatrice Cenci, principal figure in one of the most sensational Roman trials, who, aided by her lover and step-mother, had murdered her father and in 1599 was beheaded in front of the Castel Sant'Angelo. Again and again she has inspired the imagination of painters and poets. The church is rich in art treasures, even though Raphael's

FONTANA DI TREVI
(Trevi is a corruption of the Italian
word "trivio", meaning cross-roads),
Rome's most imposing fountain, was
built by Nicolò Salvi (1699–1751)
who used designs by Bernini. He
killed himself before it was finished
in 1762.

Transfiguration is no longer there; it was taken away by Napoleon and later returned to the Vatican. In the courtyard, where according to late medieval legends, Saint Peter was crucfied, is a small circular temple, a jewel of Renaissance architecture and model of structural perfection, the Tempietto of Bramante. This unique work of art seems to suffuse the Spanish severity of the courtyard with almost inspired harmony.

Built about the same time as the Acqua Paola and by the same Pope, was the Fontanone di Paolo V, also in Trastevere, but in the valley opposite the Ponte Sisto, and only half a century ago transferred to its

FONTANA PAOLA
("ACQUA PAOLA"),
*built in 1612 by Giovanni Fontana
and Carlo Maderna under Pope
Paul V.*

present site on the bank; yet it stands there as though intended for no other setting. A wide open stairway leads up to a kind of shrine. Below to the right and left two dragons, heraldic symbols of the Borghese Family, spurt their jets of water with tremendous force so that they meet in front in the centre of the lower basin. Looked at from the side they resemble two sword blades locked in passionate combat. The roaring of the water is so powerful that it drowns the din of the nearby traffic.

Typically Roman in its setting, is the Fontanone built in the late Renaissance by Pope Sixtus V opposite the church of Santa Maria della Vittoria, with copies of four Egyptian lions from the Vatican Museum. Dominating this fountain is the commanding figure of Moses in the central niche ordering the rock to open

Page 61

FOUNTAIN IN FRONT OF THE CHURCH OF SANTA SABINA. The water pours into an ancient marble tub from the mouth of a bearded man whose head is surrounded by a shell.

Page 62/63

THE ISOLA TIBERINA was dedicated to Aesculapius in ancient times. On the site of the temple of Aesculapius we now find the church of San Bartolomeo, built in the 10th century, with a Romanesque belfry. The island is linked with the river bank by the Ponte Fabricio, now the oldest bridge in Rome (64 B.C.), which is also known as the "Bridge of the four heads" because of its quadrangular pillars surmounted by a bust of Hermes.

Page 64

THE RIVER FOUNTAIN in the centre of the Piazza Navona is one of Lorenzo Bernini's finest works, executed by him and his pupils 1647–50. The four river statues under the obelisk represent the four quarters of the globe: Danube (Europe), Ganges (Asia), Nile (Africa) and, shown in our illustration, Rio de la Plata (America).

Page 65

VIEW THROUGH THE COLUMNS OF THE TEMPLE OF VESTA, built in the time of Augustus in the classical Greek style; in the background the Piazza Bocca della Verità and the Campanile of the church of Santa Maria in Cosmedin, with an 18th-century fountain of tritons in front.

Page 66/67

THE ARCHES OF THE AQUEDUCTS dominate the scenery of the Campagna plains near the Via Appia. The oldest of the aqueducts, called Acqua Claudia after the censor Appius Claudius, was built in 312 B.C. With the remains of the Acqua Marcia its arches form the Acqua Felice, restored under Pope Sixtus V, which still supply the city with 5 million gallons of water daily.

Page 68

LARGE FOUNTAIN in front of Santa Maria in Trastevere, built in 1694 after the designs of Carlo Fontana. The church which was probably the first Christian building officially opened for the cult under Constantine, was rebuilt by Innocent II in 1140. It is the first Roman church dedicated to the Virgin Mary and contains the much venerated medieval image of the Madonna del Carmine.

Page 69

FOUNTAIN OF THE TORTOISES (Fontana delle Tartarughe), one of the most delightful of Roman fountains, built in 1585 by Taddeo Landini.

Page 70/71

FONTANA DI TREVI, the most imposing fountain of Rome and a masterpiece of Baroque architecture. Clement XII commissioned Nicolò Salvi to build the grandiose affair. The architect who committed suicide before it was completed in 1762, used the designs made by Bernini a century earlier to expand the original simple basin constructed by Leone Battista Alberti who had been commissioned by Pope Sixtus IV. The facade of the Palazzo Poli forms a background to the fountain. It is supplied by the "Acqua Virgo" which Agrippa had brought to Rome for his Baths in 19 B.C.

Page 72

FOUNTAIN OF A GIRL IN THE VIA GIULIA, one of the numerous Roman fountains of unknown origin. Its sad beauty touches every passer-by.

and the water to flow forth. But how uninspired appears this violent posture when we compare it with Michelangelo's Moses in the aisle of the church of San Pietro in Vincoli, that marvellous representation of strength which impresses by its mere existence and has no need of any spectacular setting, although unfortunately it is part of a larger sculpture of lesser value. It is said that the Fontanone's designer, Prospero Bresciano, died of chagrin over the failure of his work. What lies behind this story we do not know, but it speaks well of the artist; many of his colleagues, before and since, have preened themselves complacently in front of lesser achievements.

Unique among Roman fountains, suggestive rather of northern Europe, is a pretty little fountain in the Via Lata, Wide Street, a name hardly applicable any longer to the present narrow thoroughfare. From the wall of a house the upper part of a man's body, a cap on his head, juts out pressing a longish barrel to his chest from which water pours forth as though the container were full of holes. The weather-beaten nose is damaged and at dusk the head appears like a dead man's skull. There is another jolly fountain at the Palazzo della Sapienza, seat of the old university of Rome: Two jets of water spurting from four big volumes decorated with scholarly emblems – they may symbolize the four faculties – and between them a stag's head which links up with the church of the saintly hunter Eustachio nearby. This fountain together with the graceful tower in the shape of a snail, over the Sapienza dome, reminiscent of a little pagoda, seems intended somewhat to mitigate a young student's first horrors of academic learning.

I have never been able to share the widespread enthusiasm for the fountain shaped like a barque, designed by Bernini's father, at the foot of the Spanish steps. It reminds me of an incident when the Tiber went over its banks and carried one of its boats all the way to the Piazza di Spagna. But in this case the effect misfires because the barque, as though driven into the ground, rises only a little above the level of the street. The character of a boat is much more happily preserved at the Navicella on the Coelian hill, and also, in the decoration of the ceiling of the old church Santa Maria Domenica that is behind it. The Navicella is the copy of one of those little marble boats which travellers used to dedicate to the gods as thanksgivings for their safe return from hazardous voyages. On a square pedestal of the same length as its keel, the ship rises from the water, the bow with the boar's head pointing north towards the city in the direction of the Colosseum, Nero's Golden House, the Piazza del Quirinale and the Villa Borghese. Quite charming is the fountain of Santa Maria in Cosmedin. Two mythical beings with fish-tails soar out of the rocks carrying in their raised hands a basin adorned with the crest of Pope Clement XI. The two figures seem to want to separate but they are united by their common burden. This fountain is fortunate in its position in a particularly attractive, typically Roman setting, with the Tiber in the background. Encompassed in a small area there are ancient and Christian memories; they merge with one another and impressively reveal the rise of Christianity from the ancient world, but also the fusion of antiquity with Christianity.

Santa Maria in Cosmedin which with its seven-storeyed campanile has one of the most beautiful bell-towers of Rome, was built on the ruins of a temple of

AT THE PIAZZA BOCCA
DELLA VERITÀ
*lies the little Temple of Vesta
surrounded by 20 fluted Corinthian
columns, opposite the church of
Santa Maria in Cosmedin.*

Hercules. It is popularly known also as "Bocca della Verità", Mouth of Truth, derived from a large marble disc in the portico of the church, representing a crude human face with the mouth open, reminiscent of a distant Barbarian age. The left eye over the gaping mouth seems blinded. The disc is believed to have served as a lid in an ancient Turkish bath, the steam was being released through the eyes, mouth and nose. According to the legend, people were required to put their right hand in the monster's mouth to affirm the truth of a statement. The mouth would close over the hand of a liar. I only dared putting my walking stick inside and drew it out undamaged.

The pretty little round temple opposite was formerly regarded as a sanctuary of the virgin goddess Vesta, perhaps because of the charm of the building. Nearby there are pine trees with their characteristic round tops, and one might well think suddenly to have come across

nature's original model for the ancient round temple. The sacred soil extended as far as the shadow cast by one of these hallowed trees. Close by, next to the theatre of Marcellus is the church of San Nicola in Carcere, built on the site of an old temple and from its remains; but first we come to the sanctuary of Fortuna Virilis preserved almost intact from pre-imperial times. If the belief is true that it was formerly dedicated to the Mater Matuta, the motherly goddess of dawn, there

is meaning in its transformation into a church of Our Lady. It is one of the few cases of which it can be said that there has been a direct change from temple into church. More often the retrospective view seems to indicate an organic and natural evolution.

For many, the most delightful Roman fountain is the Fontana delle Tartarughe, in the Piazza Mattei. Not long ago a bold attempt to steal the figures could fortunately be prevented. Long may these four youths,

75

supported by the heads of dolphins, continue to shove their tortoises to drink from the edge of the bowl above!

At the Fontana del Tritone in Piazza Barberini, Bernini has made delightful and bold play with the laws of gravity. As in his most famous fountain, in Piazza Navona, where four separate sculptures evolve into a single unit higher up, so here the heads of four dolphins form the base of the fountain. Their tails raised vertically, carry the scalop shell basins, and above them the sitting triton lifts a snail-shaped shell. The mere sight of it raises one's spirit. The fountain always reminds me of that curious Russian legend of the world resting upon three fishes. Indeed, anyone as

76

familiar with fish as Lorenzo Bernini might well have placed the globe upon them!

The longish Piazza Navona has retained the form which the Emperor Domitian gave the stadium and race course built there at his command. Three foun-tains are the chief features of this glorious piazza. The one on the north side is modern. Its creator did well to keep to traditional forms dangerous though this often proves to be, but nothing would have been more fitting for this square. The southern fountain, famous for the gay, lively, apparently effortless and playful figure of a Moor blowing on his conch, suggests Bernini's hand. And, then, as the climax, the fountain with the obelisk in the centre.

Lorenzo Bernini was the king of artists of the Roman Baroque, inexhaustible in his creative power as well as brilliant and, indeed, super-abundant ideas. He was a master of all the arts including that of the theatre and practised them all with passion. Whatever he did was on the grand scale, and the same can be said of Urban VIII, prototype of the masterful princely patron of the Baroque age. Bernini was his protegé, friend and companion and, to honour him, showered the three bees of the Barberini crest over the churches, palaces, and fountains of Rome. "It may be very fortunate for the artist", Urban is supposed to have said, "that Barberini has become Pope, but it is even more furtunate for Barberini that Lorenzo lived in his pontificate." Urban VIII was relatively young, fifty-five, when he became Pope, and he reigned for twenty-one years. His successor, Innocent X, Pamphili, at first neglected Bernini, but eventually was won over by the design for the obelisk fountain. One of the many Roman anecdotes about artists, which originated in the days of Vasari, tells how this came about. Bernini's friends seized the opportunity of the wedding of Innocent's niece to approach the Pope in his festive mood and show him the design which Bernini had prepared. Full of admiration, Innocent commissioned Bernini to build the fountain. The artist survived him to serve four succeeding Popes and died in 1680, aged eighty-two.

The four-fold division of the lower structure is justified by the four river gods, Danube, Ganges, Nile and Rio de la Plata. Why does Nile hide his face? In order not to have to look at the facade of Sant'Agnese, as the traditional jest has it. But the way he holds his head would rather imperil his having to stare at the dull facade of San Giacomo, which might indeed cause anyone to look away, though, at the time when Bernini built his fountain, it did not have the same form as today. However, Sant'Agnese, too, was only built after the fountain. It is also said that the figures of Nile and Rio de la Plata lifted their arms so as to protect themselves from flying masonry, as the collapse of the two towers of Sant'Agnese was, according to mischievous critics, to be expected at any moment. But there is another explanation for the raised arms, for, according to the original design, each of the four river gods was to have carried a shield with coats-of-arms. The background to all these jokes is undoubtedly the hostility between Bernini and his great rival, Borromini, the architect of that facade that deserves admiration for being inserted, so elegantly, somewhat withdrawn and with the emphasis of the two new side towers, into the front of the Palazzo Pamphili. But still, why does Nile cover his face? The explanation normally offered that the source of the Nile was not known at that time strikes me as somewhat far fetched. With equally good reason it could be said that he mourns the removal from his home land of the obelisk facing him. The real answer is probably the basic Baroque idea of the fountain. The four continents, represented by the four river gods, are paying homage to the church and to the papacy and the same time also to the person of the reigning Pope in front of whose family palace the fountain was erected. Africa as the continent least illuminated as yet by the light of the Gospel appears

TEMPLE OF CASTOR
AND POLLUX
at the Roman Forum, built in
484 B.C. by Aulus Postumius in
honour of the Dioscuri who,
according to legend, miraculously
appeared at the Battle of Lake
Regillus, thus securing the Roman
victory over the Tarquinians and
their Latin allies.

half veiled. Nevertheless, the Nile's movement may suggest the lifting of that veil that was anticipated.

Fountains and springs reach down into the depth of the earth into mystery and life-giving darkness. Springs are sacred, capable both of healing and sanctification. Near the Forum Romanum is preserved the sacred water basin of Juturna the goddess of fountains. It was at her spring that Castor and Pollux, the Dioscuri, were said to have watered their horses after the battle of Lake Regillus. The temple built next to the Lacus Juturnae commemorates the support of the "Heavenly Twins" which secured the Roman victory over the Tarquins and their Latin allies. Three Corinthian columns remain and testify to the excellence of what is perhaps the most noble and delicate, indeed, gayest piece of Roman architecture. The cult of the Romans for the two divine horsemen goes back to their appearance at the sacred spring, unless, by reversing cause and effect, one might say that the Roman cult of the Dioscuri created this tradition for its own justification. These

two heroes of Rome may remind us of the twins Romolus and Remus and of the circumstance that one of the Dioscuri proved as mortal as Remus, perhaps also symbolizing an act of expiation.

It is easier in Rome, that city of continuity, than elsewhere to reject the widely popular belief that the rise of Christianity constituted an abrupt break with the culture of the past rather than its fulfilment. The new faith did not destroy what was good in antiquity but readily adapted and transfigured it. In this way the notion of the sacredness and sanctity of water was retained. Only some little distance from the pool of Juturna and the temple of the Dioscuri, between the Arch of Septimius Severus and the Forum of Caesar is the Mamertine Prison, an ancient well-house later turned into dungeons. This gloomy place witnessed the suffering and death of many, among them, Vercingetorix, the Gallic chieftain; Jugurtha the Numedian king and the traitor Sejanus, prefect of Praetorians under the Emperor Tiberius, also Jewish rebels, Roman Senators fallen from power and Christian martyrs. It was the place for all those designated by that dangerous and ambiguous formula as "enemies of the Roman people". According to the legend, the well was a result of Saint Peter's imprisonment. It is said that the water rose miraculously to enable the Apostle to baptize the jailers whom he had converted. There is another legend connected with the spring in the open country beyond the Basilica of St. Paul, at what is today the Trappist Monastery Tre Fontane, allegedly the site of Saint Paul's execution. His severed head, it is believed, bounced three times as it rolled across the ground, and three springs welled up, one hot, one tepid and one cold. These three springs are today enclosed by a church, which in its turn has been joined with two others to complete the sacred number three. The area had long been infested by malaria and was uninhabited. French Trappist monks, to whom Pius IX gave the abbey in 1868, drained the ground and planted eucalyptus trees which absorbed the moisture. Surprisingly these foreign trees became acclimatized and a common feature in Roman gardens. The hills above the Abbey are now a dense forest and the white-flecked trunks grow to amazing heights. The oblong, hard spear-shaped leaves diffuse a strong and healing aroma. If one chews one of the leaves the taste will stay in the mouth for hours. The monks of Tre Fontane produce a fragrant liqueur from the eucalyptus fruit and leaves. The soil at the foot of the trees is now covered with green shrubs and when walking through the wood one seems to be walking on a thick carpet sown with the seeds of monastic silence. Deep furrows remind one that it was here that the Romans dug for pozzolana. This volcanic ash mixed with lime, produced the cement which ensured the durability of the buildings of Rome.

Until the close of Constantine's century only the water that flowed in the Lateran Basilica's Baptistery was used for baptism and this chapel retains to this day a privileged status. Baptisms may generally only be administered in parish churches, but two Roman churches, Saint Lateran as the city Cathedral and Saint Peter's as the centre of the Universal Church enjoyed special privileges in this respect. During the Second World War and afterwards many non-Christian American soldiers were baptized in the Lateran Baptistery or in the adjoining Portico di San Venanzio, under the Byzantine mosaics of the Blessed Virgin represented here in the ancient manner without the child and with

TEMPLE OF NEPTUNE,
probably the temple of Hadrian,
built by Antoninus Pius in 145 A.D.*,
today the Roman Stock Exchange.

her hands outstretched in prayer. One of the marvels in the richly decorated Baptistery's side chapels appeals to the ears as well as to the eyes. It is the bronze doors, donated by Pope Hilary in the fifth century, which resound musically when opened. It is said that the melodious tune is due to the doors' gold and silver inlays. Dante in the IX Canto of the *purgatorio* refers to the initial grating and groaning of the hinges which subsequently turns into sweet music.

From the outside the polygonal building looks low and squat, but on entering one is surprised by the sense of lofty heights and slenderness which it conveys. This is because of the octangular, two-storeyed structure of the columns which separate the marble centre with the actual baptismal front from the outer passage. High above in the dome is the Dove of the Holy Spirit, silver on a golden background. The font, an ancient bath tub of green basalt, has a cover, the top of which forms a papal tiara. Legend has it that this is the scene of the baptism of Constantine. It is remarkable how profoundly the personality of this first Christian Emperor has impressed itself on the imagination of the Roman people, being still today considered one of the Fathers of Christian Rome, although he was much more concerned with other parts of his empire, especially the East. The ancient floor of the Baptistery, some six feet beneath the present one, has been largely uncovered. We can clearly recognize the remains of the baths and of the heating apparatus which formed the origin of the Baptistery, thus connecting the most venerable of Roman baptismal fonts with the tradition of antiquity.

Yet many more Roman links with water, boats, fountains and fish and their symbolic significance could be listed. There is for instance the Giotto mosaic in the porch of Saint Peter's representing Jesus walking on the waters and the barque of Peter; the sails are filled with the wind and seem to break out of the flat surface. It is a landmark in the development of European art, like the Crucifixion in the chapel of Saint Catherine in San Clemente, ascribed to Masaccio, which was especi-

ally admired and studied by Michelangelo. We might recall the significance of the great fish of Jonah as the sign or type of Christ's death and resurrection on early Christian sarcophagi and burial places. There is the artificial lake north-east of Sant'Andrea della Valle, the scene of Nero's nocturnal orgies until the mad Emperor had a lake of his own built on the site where later the Colosseum was erected. There is also the Temple of Neptune which is now the Roman Stock Exchange. Unfortunately modern scholars have cast doubts on the original name of this building. One could have imagined no one more suitable than the god of the sea as the patron saint of the eddying tide of financial booms and slumps. We might take our leave from the waters of Rome with a thought for some of the holy water spouts which took the place of the early Christian "Canthari" as cleansing fountains in church porches. I am thinking in particular of the two basins of coloured inlaid marble carried by infant angels in Santa Maria Sopra Minerva, of the fishes at the base of the stoups in the church of Santa Croce, and of my favourite one, the charming marble basin in Tre Fontane. Its oval shape is reminiscent of a ship and four slim fishes at the bottom seem to be wriggling in the water as if they were alive.

THE TOMBS OF ROME

Wells and graves have always seemed to me as the two poles of man's existence. That they belong together is amply borne out by those numerous Roman wells with an ancient sarcophagus serving as their basin, and by those ancient bath tubs which later were turned into coffins.

It is part of the ambiguity of earthly life that death signifies both annihilation and infinite duration. That which is ended has been eliminated from the ever changing present, which constitutes the very texture of life, and is no longer subject to change. What death has sealed takes on its shape and finality. That achievement outlasts the grave – *vivit post funera virtus* – will be recognized in Rome by those who are receptive for it; and that all transient things are merely parables, that, too, is nowhere else so self-evident. Why not then regard Rome, that city of continuity, also and in a special sense as the city of the dead, commanding as she does over so many past ages, being the very centre of indestructable life? Apostles, martyrs, saints, spiritual and worldly rulers have found their rest as well as their memorials in Rome. To list all the famous dead would fill a volume. In some places the city of the dead lies direct under the thin layer upon which there is bustling life. Not many feet separate one from the other. The Forum Romanum, life centre of antiquity, was origin-

ally an area of graves. An old tribal shrine is supposed to lie under the tomb of Romulus. Some of the churches of Rome were originally designed as sepulchral places for shelter or defence. If we refrain from a too literal interpretation of the popular opinion, somewhat deviating as it does from the historical evidence, we might agree that, in the ages of persecution, divine worship went down into the catacombs and was there preserved.

According to a very early law, all burials within the walls were prohibited. Bodies or ashes of the dead had to be interred outside; yet in their respect for their ancestors, the Romans wanted their dead to be near at hand. Thus arose the memorials on both sides of the roads that from the gates led into Rome, and the busiest traffic passed them by. Even the families of the Emperors accepted this custom. There are three imperial memorials, not part of the city when they were built, which more than others have preserved their dignity.

West of the present day Corso, towards the Tiber, Augustus had a mausoleum built for himself, his family and successors. It was a rotunda with ascending terraces planted with cypress trees and a statue of the architect on top. The entrance was flanked by two obelisks; one of them now stands in Piazza del Quirinale, and the other in Piazza Santa Maria Maggiore. The Mau-

THE MAUSOLEUM
OF AUGUSTUS,
*built in 28 B.C. for the members of
the Julia-Claudia family, lay in
ruins at the time when Piranesi made
this engraving.*

soleum was used until the reign of Nerva, that is, up to the end of the first century A.D. It was later plundered by the Goths and in the Middle Ages the Colonna family turned it into a fortress. In the sixteenth century it became a public garden, and, in more recent times, a theatre, and finally a concert hall. The original lay-out was obliterated by a maze of small buildings, but what is left of it can now be seen as it used to be, and cypress trees are growing on it again. Undoubtedly the clearing of the site was a worthy tribute to the founder of the Empire, but to rejoice in it is difficult as in the case of the opening up of the approach to St Peter's, an even worse perpetration for which Mussolini was also responsible. The gaps were quickly filled by buildings in the style of the Fascist era, red brick faced with a coat of white travertine, devoid of ideas wanting to impress by monumental grandeur, but achieving only a barrack-like monotony. Rome

84

has been much disfigured by this type of architecture, particularly in the formerly so delightful parts, south and sout-east of the Theatre of Marcellus.

Very different has been the fate of the other tomb of the Roman emperors. The huge monument which Hadrian, taking the tomb of Augustus as his model, erected on the right bank of the Tiber, had already served as a fortress at the time of the Barbarian invasions. For centuries it dominated the river crossing, protected the Vatican and more than once also the popes. No wonder then that many popes were anxious to extend and strengthen the Castel Sant'Angelo linked through a walled passage with their residence. The monument owes its name and the angel's statue at the top to Rome's miraculous deliverance from a plague in the sixth century. Pope Gregory the Great was leading a penitential procession from the Lateran to St Peter's when, suddenly, according to the chronicler, an angel appeared above the monument, sheathing his sword and thus announcing the end of the plague, which, in fact, ceased to spread. With its vaults, palatial rooms decorated with frescoes, courtyards, ramparts, bastions and fortifications, but also with its dank dungeons, the Castel Sant'Angelo still reveals all the phases of its varied history. Famous men and women whose lives have thrilled the world ever since were among the prisoners: the unhappy Beatrice Cenci, the great Benvenuto Cellini, sculptor and braggart, the incomparable Cagliostro who, with incredible impudence knew how to charm and exploit his Rococo contemporaries, so proud of their enlightened age and yet so easily duped by him.

The Emperor Constantine, great builder of Roman churches, preferred his own city Constantinople, the old Byzantium, to Rome and was buried there. His mother, Helena, however, and his daughters, Constance and Helena, have their tombs in Rome. Constantine built, or at least contributed to what is known as the work of his daughter Constance, the church of Sant'Agnese fuori le mura, between Porta Pia and the bridge over the river Aniene at the foot of Monte Sacro. There St Agnes, beheaded in the circus of Domitian, the present Piazza Navona, is honoured as a patron of virginal purity normally, also perhaps in harmony with her name, she is represented with an *agnus,* a little lamb. Her church is built over catacombs, the high altar stands exactly over her grave, a cultic justification, as it were, of the original purpose of the catacombs. In the cloister outside a remarkable event is recorded by a large fresco. On the occasion of a visit to this church in 1855 by Pius IX, who was greatly attached to it, the floor in one of the side chapels suddenly collapsed, and the Pope and those who were with him fell into the vault beneath, though without injuring themselves. The picture illustrates the terrible decadence into which Italian painting had fallen by the middle of the last century. How differently would such an event have been recorded in the ages of the great popes, connoisseurs and patrons of the arts; but for the unfortunate accident, this representation almost evokes ridicule.

A mighty staircase leads down into the church which lies below street level; at the Western entrance it borders on a lovely green garden, appropriately so for the virgin patron with the lamb. The high altar is surmounted by a canopy on four porphyry pillars, and supports the antique statue of a pagan goddess which, with the mere addition of a new alabaster head, was restored as St Agnes – another expression of characteristic Roman continuity. Near the sacristy is the entrance to the catacombs, the dampness of which has damaged the frescoes of Sant'Agnese and of the neighbouring churches. In descending one is given a candle and has to shield the flickering flame from the draught. The catacombs of Sant'Agnese, containing some eight thousand graves, lack artistic decoration, but more than any other catacombs they give an impression of the original conditions. Endless seem the dark passages, in the niches of which, one above the other, the bodies of the dead were placed. The tomb stones of the earliest times bore no other inscription save that of the person's name, with the occasional addition of the words "in pace" – in peace. Whatever else was to be conveyed was expressed in the language of images and symbols, such as a fish to mark the tomb of a believer in Christ, or a dove carrying a wreath as a sign of innocence. In these catacombs a great deal can be discovered that tells us realistically of every day life long ago, such as for instance the artless carving of a ham on a butcher's grave. Next to Sant'Agnese is the mausoleum of Constance and Helena, converted into the church of Santa Costanza in the Middle Ages, a round building of the type favoured by Roman mausoleum architecture. It stands over catacombs which are reputed to be the oldest in Rome and was probably originally designed as the side chapel of a large basilica, the elliptical ground plan of which can still be traced in the gardens. The interior, with cupola, double columns and a passage way encircling it on a lower level, wholly reflects the time of its origin. It contains the precious and the oldest known Christian mosaics, in part an ornamental play of colours and lines, in part an intricate pattern of plant, animal and figurative motifs. Again and again there are the motifs of grape harvest and peacocks. The old colours have retained their golden splendour to this day. The themes seem to be of antique origin, as though the early Christian era had not as yet been able to develop artistic forms more appropriate to the tombs of Constantine's daughters. Even so, these designs, too, have their Christian symbolism, the peacock suggests immortality and self evident is of course the meaning of Psyche taken up into Olympus.

There are more than forty catacomb sites in Rome. The oldest date back to the first century A.D.; burial in and near churches was unknown before the fourth century. The history of the catacombs illustrates also, and significantly, the development from family burial grounds to the parish cemetery. The great majority of the catacombs lie in the southern part of the city outside Porta San Sebastiano. This may have been due to the composition of the soil no less than to the proximity of the Via Appia and its associations with Roman burial traditions.

The Via Appia, the oldest of the military roads leaving the city, was built by the Censor Appius, the architect also of the first Roman aqueduct, the Aqua Appia. It was known as the queen of roads, but one could regard it as a widowed queen, justifying her royal dignity also as a road of tombs.

Still within the limits of the Aurelian, but outside the Servian wall are the *Columbaria* which have been preserved extensively. The Latin name, signifying pigeon-house, suggests the shape and purpose of these burial places for cinerary urns; to save space, they were laid close to one another into tiers of niches. This was the way in which the poor and the slaves were buried

SANTA COSTANZA,
*a round church erected in the
4th century by Constantine as a
mausoleum for his daughters
Constance and Helena.*

and it may remind one of their jerry-built tenement dwellings. But there is another explanation which touches upon the transforming and purifying effect of fire. Ceasar's body was consumed by the flames on the Forum Romanum and Augustus built a temple on the site. The ashes, not the bodies, of the Emperor Hadrian and his family were interred in the vaults of Castel Sant'Angelo and this at a time when burials and sarcophagi were becoming more frequent, especially among the upper classes who, true to their conserva-

87

THE APPIAN WAY
*was the road of tombs of ancient
Rome. The ruins on this Piranesi
engraving are described as the
monuments of Piso Licinianus and
of the Cornelia family.*

tive outlook, took up again the older custom. Apart from Egypt the Jews were the only people of the ancient world who rejected cremation outright. In following them, the Christians adhered to the practice of earth burial but, when the ground was suitable, preferred to lay their dead in rock graves in imitation of their Saviour.

The return to earth burial was responsible for the growth of a third art form of Roman origin besides the construction of vaults and portrait sculpture; this was the carving of sarcophagi. Its evidence can be found everywhere in Rome. It is a form of relief art using ornamental, representational, but also mythological and even topical motifs and is closely linked with the ornamental reliefs on triumphal arches and columns. It has produced great artistic creations, but also a vast amount of second-rate stereotyped works. And in this connection I must ask the reader to accept a confession. I have come to Rome, not as an art historian, but as a lover of this city, and I must openly admit never to be able to touch any sarcophagi, even of inferior workmanship, without a feeling of reverence and satisfaction. In some way all of them are linked with the whole of antiquity and like those Roman busts of decadent periods reflect the glory of that world. An instantaneous confrontation with my mind and heart takes place, just as any sentence, however meaningless, from a book of elementary Latin suggests to me the clarity, dignity and force of that beloved language. And the same happens – I trust art historians will pardon me – when I look at the mosaics of the early Christian centuries and of the early Middle Ages. I am able to recognize, and indeed know from books the variations in style, I am aware that at a certain moment life began to fade from these colourful, glittering creations leaving them in solemn rigidity until Pietro Cavallini and Jacopo Torriti in the thirteenth century recaptured the lost reality, and became harbingers of a new flowering of painting.

But to me the mosaics of the eight and ninth centuries no less than those of the early Christian era suggest the dim golden glimmer of a supernatural faith which not only affects the onlooker but carries him away; their very stiffness, angularity and clumsiness remind me that salvation came to us from the East, as this art form came from Byzantium. I know that this sort of thing sounds childish and should not be said among scholars, but I admit to it, frankly and *entre nous,* trusting that some kind of understanding may have developed between the reader and the author, as in an exchange of Roman memories over a glass of wine.

The Via Appia at first runs between walls. Its character is suburban, but suburban in the sense of announcing the country-side rather than the humdrum activities of the city to which suburbs usually like to cling. Beyond the little stream Almone, almost imperceptibly, fragments of tombs begin to appear. To the left lies the chapel Domine Quo Vadis, formerly called "Ubi apparuit dominus" – where the Lord appeared. It marks the site of the most moving of early Christian legends, Peter leaving Rome, meeting Jesus and then returning to the city to face martyrdom. Soon afterwards there are cypress trees, those tall symbols of eternal rest which the ancient world has also bequeathed to our northern European cemeteries. They dominate the road, and only occasionally are replaced by pine trees. The surroundings take on a more rural character, we meet flocks of sheep, there is a smell of manure and fields. Farm houses, some of them embedded into the remains of ancient tombs, border the road. The old sepulchral church of San Sebastiano owes its preservation and the restoration of its Baroque facade, as so many Roman churches do, to Cardinal Scipio Borghese, the great collector, and patron of the arts, a friend of Bernini's. Behind San Sebastiano the road descends to that low area from which the catacombs derived their name, for "ad catacumbas" means a place near a ravine-like lowland. When the road again ascends, at the site of the chariot race course of Maxentius, there is the round tomb of Caecilia Metella, daughter-in-law of Crassus the triumvir. Only a family of Crassus' pro-

THE CHURCH
OF SAN SEBASTIANO,
*one of the seven basilicas included in
the "Pilgrimage of the Seven
Churches", dates from before the
5th century, the present form from
1614.*

verbial wealth could afford such a monument for one of their women. It looks like a migthy bulwark and in fact it served as a fortress in the Middle Ages until under Sixtus V who decisively checked the belligerent and unruly Roman patricians it became part of the Appian ruins.

Ruins now dominate the road. There is more solitude and grandeur. Tomb stone follows upon tomb stone. It was thus far that the stream of lava flowed down from the Alban hills in prehistoric times. Under foot there are still traces of the ancient lava pavement which in Rome is now only found around the Forum Romanum and the Palatine. Some of the ruins have taken on mushroom-like shapes. The inhabitants of the neighbourhood helped themselves to whatever bricks they needed and left these thin stems with a

THE VIA TIBURTINA
*connecting Rome with Tivoli. Behind
the Ponte Lucano which traverses
the Aniene lies the tomb of the
Plautus family.*

wider top. The landscape opens out, the view extends further, the outlines of the Alban hills become clearer and more tangible; on the left appear the arches of the aqueduct.

It is perhaps at sunset or by moonlight that the Via Appia reveals its secrets most readily. But even in brightest sunshine on lovely spring days or in the burning summer it preserves a grave sense of melancholy and the promise of infinite peace, Roman stoicism merging with the fervent capacity for belief of the early Christians. The genius-figure holding a torch reversed has his brow adorned equally with the laurels of ancient glory, the olive leaves of peace and the palm branches of the certainty of the resurrection.

The area of the catacombs extends from the Via Appia westwards to San Paolo fuori le mura. The most important ones are those named after the martyrs Sebastian and Callisto. For about three centuries of the Christian era the catacombs, burrowed into the sandy-coloured tuffa-rock, were the customary burial places. Contrary to the belief of the Middle Ages with their passion for relics, only a fraction of those buried there can thus have been martyrs. But already early on cultic devotion concentrated on the graves of the martyrs. The faithful gathered for memorial services, chapel-like places developed, and added to the pious inscriptions of the early era were artistic embellishments, especially frescoes but also carvings on the sarcophagi. Apart from the ordinary graves in niches, there were also, if only rarely and as marks of distinction, early sarcophagi made of marble or other stone. Here are the roots of the totality of Christian sacred art as it evolved from the artistic tradition of the ancient world.

The development was by no means a rapid one, and it indicates at the same time the transition from the offshoots of antiquity to the art of the Middle Ages. The pagan themes disappeared gradually, but the delicate lines and garland patterns of antique painting remained. Christian ideas were initially expressed in symbols as through agreed abbreviations. Birds and ships, for example, suggest the journey of the departed souls to their eternal rest. Later, painting and sarcophagus sculpture began to employ biblical motives, but the symbolic character prevailed for a long time. The artists had, as it were, first to overcome their reverent hesitation before they dared depict scenes direct from the Gospel. Even the Crucifixion. The Crucifixion was at first represented merely by the image of Isaac's sacrifice, just as the often repeated story of Jonah signified the Resurrection. Finally representations of the Eucharistic meal appeared, of the feeding of the five thousand, the resurrection of Lazarus, and the good shepherd.

If you have the opportunity of seeing the catacombs not only with a crowd of tourists but can get to know them more intimately, such an experience will be one of the most precious Roman memories. I recall a solemn Mass on the feast day of Saint Cecilia at the grave of this martyr in the catacombs of San Callisto. She had lain here for six hundred years, then her sarcophagus was taken to the church in Trastevere into her original home, also the site of her martyrdom, had been transformed. The participants of that service underground, priests, laymen, a choir of some forty young clerics, gathered near the entrance to the catacombs in the old Oratorium Sancti Callisti in Arenariis and in procession all descended. Palm branches decorated the entrance and suddenly this ancient symbol of peace had the full dignity and force of a contemporary event. Below ground, in a narrow space lit by candles, close to the graves of the popes from the ages of persecution, the divine mysteries were celebrated. How very different the words of the Gospel about the foolish virgins and their oil lamps sounded in this place where the little clay lamps had always been in use. I remember the celebrating priest, a tall good-looking young Italian, his resonant voice, his movements typical of the southerner, full of vitality yet dignified in a Roman way. His sermon was both inspiring and profound. The Mass was celebrated in the severe, traditional style. Some of the singers – there was not enough space for all of them in the chapel – stood in an adjacent passage

SAN PAOLO FUORI
LE MURA
*(St Paul without the walls), the
most spacious church in Rome after
St Peter's, on the site of the tomb
of St Paul where Constantine built a
small church.*

way, invisible to the rest of us. Some chants were sung by them alone, not by the rest of the choir, and their voices seemed to rise up from the nether world.

The road leading to Ostia, like the Via Appia, is bordered with graves. It was here, according to a credible tradition, that St Paul was buried in pre-catacomb times. Constantine had already built a shrine over his grave, transformed by his successors into the noblest of Roman basilicas. Its significance was not even diminished after the re-building of St Peter's. The great fire of July 11th 1823, started by the carelessness of some workmen on the roof, in barely six hours destroyed the greater part of the building. Pope Pius VII then lay dying and was never told about the disaster. Earthquakes and floodings of the Tiber had left their marks on the Basilica before this catastrophe,

93

and in 1891 the new building, that had been completed in the middle of the century, was severely damaged by an explosion in a gun-powder magazine near-by. After such disasters it is understandable that few important works of art are left at San Paolo, apart from the magnificent medieval paschal candle-stick, the tabernacle and some mosaics. The basilica impresses with its time-honoured dignity, purity and dimensions that shun all other adornment. In the five parts of the nave there is not a single chapel or monument nor added structures; all these have been placed, though sparingly in the transept. St Paul's is the largest church in Rome after St Peter's. Something of St Peter's Roman brightness and majesty also overwhelms those who enter here. And the very vastness of this church inevitably seems to point to the great teacher of the nations, who was the first to show the way of the Gospel to the nations of the world, and the first to go upon it himself. It was from St Paul's that Gregory XI entered Rome in 1377, thus ending the exile of the Popes at Avignon. Above the columns there is a long row of papal portraits in medallion-like form. An ominous prophecy fortells that there is room only for very few more portraits, and that thus the end of the world is near. You can see for yourself that there is plenty of room left. The area in front of St Paul's is without character. Looking towards Rome from here all you can see is the periphery of a newly built modern industrial city. Until the early Middle Ages the basilica was linked with the Porta Ostiensis by a roofed colonnade; the broken remains are lying in the grass today. Similar covered passages extended the pilgrims path, with some interruptions, by way of Santa Maria in Cosmedin, San Lorenzo in Damaso and the Tiber and on to St Peter's. Accounts of such linking buildings sound almost incredible since the distance from St Paul's to the city gate is about half an hour's walk. But what remains is sufficient evidence for the vast proportion of the buildings of classical times, as for instance of the bridge which Calligula built over the Forum Romanum linking Palatine and Capitol.

Like St Paul's, St Peter's was built by Constantine over the tomb of the apostle by whose name it is known. St Peter's stands over very old burial ground, and under the crypts of the Vatican a necropolis from pagan times has recently been disoverd. The Cathedral has always been regarded as one of the principal shrines of Christendom. For six and a half centuries it was a church where emperors were crowned. The idea for an elaborate reconstruction of St Peter's excelling the old building in grandeur, could only arise after the Popes had returned from Avignon and had transferred their residence from the Lateran to the Vatican.

Much has been written, combined with a good deal of controversy, about the architectural history of St Peter's with its numerous plans, first half-agreed to, then countermanded and changed, and all the contradictory attempts to reconcile the requirements of art and religion. Any encyclopaedia or reference book will provide ample information. We may regret that the majestic dome, when seen at close quarters, seems somewhat to squat on its shoulders. One may criticize Maderna's facade for concealing the very vista it was built to enhance. But ultimately we shall always return to the impact such as only works of nature make. As it stands the gigantic building has become rooted in our consciousness, we accept it as

SAN PAOLO FUORI
LE MURA
was completely destroyed by fire in
1823 and rebuilt by 1854.

we would accept the Alps, though it might be said of them that some measure of geological rearrangement would have improved their shape. But generally speaking we cling to appearances.

Decisive for this building are the laws of space and light, and they apply equally to the square in front of it. There is no other in the world to match it. The cathedral seems to extend its two colonnades like arms opening in a world-embracing gesture. But the vast dimensions have no disturbing effect, neither on St Peter's Square nor in its interior, for besides majesty it has the serenity of true greatness, the kind of sublime loftiness that does not humiliate man but makes him share it.

The Piazza is inlaid – fittingly so for the centre of the world – with astronomical and meteorological

Page 97

THE PYRAMID OF CAIUS CESTIUS (121 ft high) outside the Porta San Paolo, formerly Porta Ostiensis. It contains the tomb of the Praetor, people's tribune, Caius Cestius who died in 12 B.C. Next to it the Protestant cemetery with the urn of P. B. Shelley, the graves of Kreats and of many other famous visitors to Rome.

Page 98/99

THE LARGE CYLINDRICAL TOWER (65 ft in diameter) of the Tomb of Caecilia Metella is one of the most imposing landmarks on the Appian Way. There is an inscription in memory of Caecilia, the daughter of Quintus Metellus Creticus, who conquered Crete, and the wife of Crassus the Younger, son of the triumvir and one of Caesar's generals in Gaul.

Page 100

A LARGE HEAD OF CONSTANTINE, remains of a colossal statue of the emperor from the Basilica of Constantine or Maxentius, now in the inner courtyard of the Palazzo dei Conservatori on the Capitol.

Page 101

THE CATACOMBS OF ST CALIXTUS are both the most important and impressive ones in Rome. Here are the tombs of the early popes St Sixtus II, St Anterus, St Fabian, St Lucius and St Eutychianus, the tomb of St Cecilia and a fresco of Christ Ruler of the World which goes back to a Byzantine model of the 4th century.

Page 102/103

THE DOME OF ST PETER'S, the most majestic of Michelangelo's creations, is the symbol of Christian Rome. It rises on the site on which Constantine in 324 A.D. erected a basilica in the form of a Latin cross over the tomb of St Peter. Towards the middle of the 15th century it was in danger of collapsing and Nicholas V decided to rebuild it. Work was begun in 1452, but not completed until 1626. Below the papal altar erected over the Confession is the entrance into the lower church with the burial place of St Peter and the tombs of several popes; above it rises the famous baldaquin which Bernini built in 1633.

Page 104

THE MOSES OF MICHELANGELO, which the sculptor made from Carrara marble (1513–1517) for the tomb of Pope Julius II, is a particular object of interest in the church of San Pietro in Vincoli.

data, a wind-rose, the signs of the zodiac and of the solstices. Marked are the two spots, seen from which the 284 columns standing in four rows so conceal one another that a single row only is visible. This seems to be one of those glorious tricks of perspective loved by the Baroque and by the great Bernini. And yet it is simply explained. St Peter's Square forms an oval and each of the two colonnades form the segment of a circle; the two spots mentioned are the centres of incomplete circles. Exactly in the middle of each colonnade there is an interruption, the columns are cut through by a path recognizable from far by a papal crest in stone on top. Each of the roof statues on the curved arms of the colonnade forms an extension of the pillar beneath it, while on the straight parts flanking the church facade the statues of saints are arranged in pairs. Nothing is left to chance or arbitrary design. The obelisk stands in the centre of the axis linking with the two interruptions in the colonnade; to the right and left of it, in but minute variation, are the two fountains. The waters rising up glisten in the sunshine with the seven colours of the rainbow or they unfold like a flower and, in a stronger breeze, spray across the Square.

The Square on the Capitol owes part of its effect to the obliquely placed facade of the palaces on either side. This feature has been taken up in front of St Peter's. The Piazza between the colonnades and the church, flanked to the right and left by out-buildings, widens imperceptibly towards the Cathedral and thus reinforces the impression of a facade rising up to an immense height. It is approached by the magnificent, most artistically and cleverly worked out stairway in the world. Not even the approaches to the choir of Santa Maria Maggiore or to the Lateran Basilica can be compared to it.

The interior of St Peter's is everywhere flooded with light entering from the tall windows. It always seems empty, always quiet and, except on great and crowded occasions, the visitor seems to be lost in its vastness. The wealth of sculpture, too, nowhere obtrudes. The four colossal statues placed in niches on pillars that support the dome have almost relief effect, and the many memorials also appear to be designed to adorn the walls rather than the interior as a whole. They are monuments, not tombs. The coffins are underneath the church in the Vatican grottos which have undergone many transformations, their lower floor formed the level of the old church of St Peter's. Chapels, passages, niches, sarcophagi, memorials and statues form an underground world of their own. There are some traces of the old church, lower still is the burial area of pagan Rome.

The dome forms the architectural centre of the church, its cultic centre is the *confessio* with its ever burning lights and the papal altar under Bernini's baldacchino with its fantastic spiral columns. The axis of the nave links up with the *Cathedra Petri,* the wooden episcopal chair of Peter enclosed in a bronze throne. It appears to be lifted up into golden clouds illuminated by rays of the Holy Spirit and is supported by the statues of the four doctors of the Church: Ambrose, Athanasius, Augustine, and John Chrysostom.

It is difficult to say which detail of St Peter's impresses itself most strongly upon our senses, indeed, how far any detail can survive separately within such an abundance. Some may carry away with them the

SAN PIETRO IN VATICANO,
*the largest of Christian basilicas
in its present form, is a work
of three architects: Michelangelo
(1475–1564), Carlo Maderna
(1556–1629), Gian Lorenzo
Bernini (1598–1680).*

impression of the red porphyry top, upon which Charlemagne received the Roman crown of Western Christendom, others may remember the much venerated bronze statue of St Peter sitting on the throne, others again the fabulous Pietà made by Michelangelo when he was twenty-five, imbued with that transfigured force of suffering that seems possible only within the Christian context, others yet again will recall the central of the five entrance doors leading from the porch into the church with their glorious carvings, and others may think of the unadorned entrance door to the right, walled up and marked with a dark cross. This is the Porta Santa, and four times each century the successor of St Peter knocks at it with a precious hammer, thus proclaiming the beginning of a Holy Year.

PIAZZA SAN PIETRO,
the masterpiece of Bernini
(1656–1667), is one of the most
famous and beautiful squares in the
world, with its 284 Doric columns.
and 140 statues on the ballustrade
which surmounts the colonnade.

Of the buildings adjoining St Peter's it can well be said that they are something of a city of their own. I should like to single out only one part of it, the foundation, which derives its name from the cemetery linked with it, the Campo Santo dei Tedeschi. The proud inscription "Carolus Magnus me fundavit" refers to the foundation of the first crowned emperor of the renewed Roman Empire. The small cemetery shaded by cypresses and palm trees carries the inscription at the entrance "Teutones in Pace". It is the oldest Christian cemetery above ground in Rome, made by Constantine and in the Middle Ages was allotted to the German speaking peoples of the Holy Roman Empire.

Another cemetery, non-Roman and yet intimately connected with Rome, received its name from the Pyramid of Cestius. It is the cemetery of foreigners, the burial place of visitors who died in Rome and is intended for non-Catholic Christians. Englishmen, Americans, Russians and Protestant Germans are buried here. The oldest part dating back to the eighteenth century, lies immediately at the foot of the Pyramid. Indescribable is the silent magic of this place. Broken marble tablets and memorials lie scattered among the tall grass and flowers, there are no enclosures for individual graves. The elegiac spirit of melancholy, purified as it was by ancient Greece and Rome, hovers over the place, and is reflected in the forms and ornaments of the graves. No Christian symbol is to be seen anywhere. In those days the Papal State forbade non-Catholic denominations the public display of the cross. This may seem strange to us living after the age of John XXIII, but we have to bear in mind that in those days Catholic services were also banned in most Protestant countries and Catholics in England were deprived even of their ordinary civil rights.

Here lies John Keats under a tomb-stone the sad inscription of which fails to mention his name, nearby his devoted Severn. The ashes of Shelley are interred near those of his friend Trelawney who had snatched the poet's heart from the flames of the funeral pyre at Viareggio. There is a grave of Robert Michael Ballantine, writer of adventure stories for boys, of the sculptor John Gibson, of the American poet and sculptor William Wetmore Story and his wife, friends of the Brownings. There are the graves of William and Mary Howitt, those industrious English writers who settled in Rome and devoted themselves to animal welfare and eucalyptus trees, of the German painters Carstens and Föhr, the English poet and critic John Addington Symonds, biographer of Shelley and translator of the sonnets of Michelangelo and Campanella. The newer part of the cemetery along the inside of the city wall, lacks the magic of the old. The graves lie close to one another as though the dead continued to share in the confines of an overpopulated world. But the dark cypress trees, the background of the Aurelian wall, a noble monument here and there, and the memory of some of these dead may reconcile us to the cemetery's less agreeable features. A grey stone placed between tall pine trees has a carved medallion of Goethe's only son August – "*Filius Goethe patri antevertens*", preceeding the father, reads the reticent inscription.

Fragments of pottery can be said to be part of the household of death. At the north-west end of the cemetery, rises barren and green at the same time, the strange formation of the Monte Testaccio, the mount of potsherds with a dark cross on the top. It was formed already in ancient times from the pieces of wine and oil pitchers, fruit and grain containers which were unloaded in the Tiber harbour nearby. The longish-shaped mount is uninhabited and untilled. As by a walled enclosure it is surrounded by a row of low buildings their backs leaning against the slope – nearly all of them wine cellars and taverns, widely diffusing the smell of wine and wine barrels. The place has remained true to the story of its origin.

The Pantheon was built by Menenio Agrippa, Augustus' son-in-law, not as a mausoleum, but as a temple dedicated to the gods of life. It was restored by Hadrian after being damaged by lightning. Here the

108

Greek and Roman worlds merge in perfect unity, the columned porch recalling Hellas, the dome-shaped rotunda Rome and Rome alone. Transformed into a Christian church, a vast quantity of martyrs' remains – twenty-eight cart loads, it was said – were brought here from the catacombs in the seventh century. Needless to say not all of these bones were those of martyrs, but the Romans used to regard as such all those buried in the catacombs. The Pantheon later became a place for state burials. It contains the

coffins of Victor Emanuel II and Umberto I, the coffins of Raphael, his assistant Giovanni da Udine and of other artists of his and later times. But it is not the graves that sanctify this place; they are sanctified by it.

The overwhelming thing about the Pantheon is its utter simplicity. One cannot attempt to imitate simplicity. Dimensions, proportions and forms have the capacity to convince through their naturalness. Even the facade has but two simple motifs: column and pediment. This is where the architects of St Peter's found their inspiration, and yet there is no affinity between the two cupolas. One gives the impression of elevation, the other of stillness. One seems to have a will of its own, the other mere existence, one seems to convey the certainty of heaven, the other of the solid and abiding earth. The circular and windowless interior derives its majestic and also liberating effect from perfect symmetry.

It is the supreme achievement of the ancient world that governs here, that absolute harmony that was to be revived once more as a wonderful expression of Italian feeling and then to disappear. There is hardly any other Roman church in which light has so successfully been made use of as a building's formative element. But the light is not refracted, as it is elsewhere, by coloured glass windows or by metal or stone ornamentation. It enters in its elemental form and overwhelms by its purity, it penetrates through the opening in the dome just as rain and snow would. The effect of the coffered ceiling as so often in Rome, can hardly be overestimated. In the ancient buildings these panels in the ceiling were filled with rosettes and other ornaments of metal or stucco and this may originally also have been the case in the Pantheon. But the Renaissance artists who revived antiquity must have felt the charm of those empty, coffered areas with nothing but their geometric effect, and thus they have sealed, both in the Pantheon and in San Bernardo the glory of cupolas with the magic of absolute space and lofty harmony. Where the cupola begins ends the coloured marble facing of the wall. Above, five rows of grey coffers from an inverted bowl. There are rhombic designs, polygonal pattern, curved lines have all been dispensed with: there are merely five rows of lacunars which grow progressively smaller as they near the central and only opening of the cupola. No more fittingly bright resting place for Raphael and his disciples could be imagined.

THE ANCIENT MONUMENTS OF ROME

"On the Capitol,
There I stand
And don't know what to do."

This rather silly verse was written by Goethe's unimaginative grand-son. The grandfather knew the answer well enough and perhaps also his father, buried at the foot of the Pyramid of Cestius. The doggerel conveys, no doubt without the writer's intention, something of the standards and norms set by the period of classical antiquity. Its very essence is embodied on the Capitoline hill.

It was the genius of Hellas to glorify man as an incorruptible being, and Rome's to express human achievement. Ancient Greece epitomized man as an individual, Rome viewed man in his social relationships as soldier, husbandman, father of a family. In his creative capacity, too, Roman man, has through time and space, conserved for us the very essence of antiquity like the flow of water chanelled through his aqueducts. The Romans shared with the Greeks a spontaneous love of life such as we associate with antiquity in general, but the Roman attitude of masculine tension contrasted with the relaxed humanity of Greece. The Roman character contained an element of sobriety, purposiveness and unemotional calculation. That was the spirit of Roman statecraft, Roman Law, of the Roman legions and of Roman philosophy with its preference for empirical, rather than speculative problems. The same spirit is also expressed in Roman art as it developed in imperial times, especially in the construction of arches. It is dominated by an unflinching will to overcome space, indeed, the laws of gravity. The Romans were not artistically gifted by nature, but the breeze that blew from Hellas had inspiring effects. Ultimately they were enriched by Eastern fervour and ardour and the resulting blend has been beneficial for our civilization.

The Roman Empire embodied the notion of everlasting world peace and rested on political foundation such as no Greek could ever have laid. The Pax Romana paved the way for the peaceful reign of Christ on earth and its heir, the Holy Roman Empire, likewise attempted to build a road towards an eternal kingdom of peace. In spite of its many blemishes this Empire managed to achieve something on these lines. Its supranational idea, at least points the way into our own future. We are entitled to muse in this way when standing on the Capitol, for it is one of the fundaments of the Western world.

On the Capitol stood the Temples of Jupiter and Juno Moneta. They have long since disappeared and

THE PIAZZA
DEL CAMPIDOGLIO
*with the Palazzo Senatorio and the
Palazzo dei Conservatori was
designed and planned by Michelangelo
and finished in the 17th century. At
the side a grand staircase leads to the
Romanesque church of Santa Maria
in Aracoeli.*

the church of Santa Maria in Aracoeli has arisen on their foundations. We should enter this church through the back door so as to be able to leave it, so to speak, unprepared by the magnificent staircase leading up to the main entrance. The view is breathtaking; we face a very ocean of expanse, freedom, light and infinitude. There are not many stairways in the world, which, when one descends them, evoke such feeling of floating on air as this one does. It was built during the period of deepest Roman decline in the years of the

112

Avignon exile, and it may be that some pledge was read into it of recapturing the greatness of Roma that seemed to have passed.

When ascending the Capitol, however, we should use the middle ramp. We shall then be confronted by the prototype of all equestrian statues ever built, the emperor Marcus Aurelius on horseback. His name is linked also with the column he erected in the Piazza Colonna, that chronicle of Roman feats of war which also serves as the oldest existing pictorial documentation of the history of the Germanic peoples. Marcus Aurelius never became a figure of legendary popularity; that was not the way of a man of his stoic self-control and imperial sense of duty. His monument, which previously stood in front of the Lateran, and was transferred to its present site only when Michelangelo re-designed the Capitol, had long been regarded as a statue of Constantine and probably owes its preservation to this error. The incomparable square owes its present shape to Michelangelo. Before his time the hill had only been accessible from the opposite side; he gave it the front facing the Campo Marzio from which the new city had arisen. He also built the beautiful stairway leading to the central of the three buildings surrounding the square, the Palace of the Senators on the site of the ancient Tabularium or State Archives. According to his plans a colossal statue of Jupiter was to have been erected. Instead of it the statue of Roma was put there, carved in the style of the imperial age like a seated Minerva, taken from a temple in a small town in the Volscian hills. In size, it is not suited to the dimensions of the square, but holding a globe and a lance, it conveys the meaning of the Capitol more fittingly than the statue of Jupiter

could have done. The fountain at her feet is surrounded by the figures of Nile and Tiber as the two most important rivers of the Roman Empire and of the Mediterranean world. The God of the Nile rests his arm upon a small sphinx, the Tiber upon a she-wolf with the two youths Romulus and Remus playing

113

THE RUINS
OF THE FORUM ROMANUM
*with the triple Arch of Septimius
Severus on the left (see also p. 117).*

beside it. The two gods are represented with cornu-copi, the ancient Roman symbol of prosperity and wealth. This is a stereotype ornament far too frequently encountered and it can become no less tiresome than the gifts which it contains. Apart from the Palatine, the Capitol is the only Roman hill which is not a residential area. In the Middle Ages it was a maze of rubbish heaps, ruins, gardens and pastures. This is recalled by the name Monte Caprino, mount of goats, and by Campo Vaccino or Bovino, cattle field, the name for the Forum at its foot. A Roman visitor like Goethe knew no other name for the Forum Romanum

VIEW FROM THE ARCH
OF TITUS
towards the Casino Farnese,
erected in the 16th century
on the slopes of the Palatine
(see also p. 6).

and it was only in the nineteenth century that it was unearthed and freed from the debris of the ages. The Forum Romanum is generally known simply as the Forum so as to emphasize its unique and privileged position also in regard to the adjoining Imperial Fori of Caesar, Augustus and Trajan. It is *the* Forum, just as Rome is *the* city.

Our view from the Capitol encompasses the whole of the Forum, the Basilica of Constantine, the Colosseum and the Palatine steep. Indeed from certain points of the slope, but especially from the steps leading to the back entrance of the Aracoeli, we can see the three imperial triumphal arches, those of Septimius Severus, Titus and Constantine.

115

The Capitol, the Forum and its neighbourhood are places where history did not just occur, but was made. Here great speeches were delivered, decisions taken, and actions glorified the effects of which are still felt by our world. Buildings of political and sacred significance stand close to each other. The two sides of Roman life which they embody are inseparable, and this is equally true of the remains standing upright or lying on the ground, those which are half preserved and those which can only be re-erected in our mind; even their ages of origin seem to merge when we look at them.

There are seasons of the year and hours of the day when it is possible to see Forum and Palatine without meeting anyone, not even those hordes of keen and noisy tourists marshalled by a guide as well versed in taking tips as in every kind of platitude. In the silvery grey veil of the winter mist at dusk or in a gentle drizzle you can wander around here by yourself and sense the mysterious melancholy of earthly life and of the tears which Virgil immortalized in verse. Under the trees on the south-western edge of the Forum in the Farnese Gardens and on the Palatine our feet rustle through leaves turned yellow. Leaving the footpath and stepping over a wire fence we find ourselves in the green wilderness that has grown around ruins that now look like rocks. There are acanthus bushes with large green leaves which sometimes cover a piece of masonry on the ground with ornamental carvings representing the very same plant. It is as though no watchman or gardener, not even an archaeologist, had ever set foot in this place, as though the bushes, trees and grass had always clad the stones with foliage as they do today.

The monuments of the Forum and Palatine date back to prehistoric times. The origins of some are difficult to determine; to these belong the tufa stone cisterns at the House of Livia, the Lapis Niger (black stone) and the oldest known, but indecipherable Latin inscription. These are relics of some distant primordial age that did not even have imagery. The consecrated site guarded the memory of a divine father figure and tribal hero and even the sober and practical minds of the Romans may have sensed here the breath of a mystery they could no longer understand. The long line of these relics ends with the still upright column of Phocas, ascribed, however, to the first century A.D. but an obsequious exarch, Smaragdus, had it adorned in the year 608 with the statue of the then governing Byzantine Emperor Phocas and an inscription. Thus the memorial of an upstart brigand marks the end of the living history of the Forum. Henceforth there is but decay, ruin, at best, indifference and ultimately scholarly restoration, interpretation and preservation. This is not to be underrated, but it does indicate that the stream of life has run dry.

Beside the Arch of Septimius Severus there are the remains of a round hollow wall marking a site where sacral and profane trends may have fused in its veneration as was often the case in ancient times. This is the *Umbilicus urbis,* the navel of the city, and in its time it was probably more than merely a topographical centre; indeed, in view of the common Roman identification of *urbs* and *orbis,* city and world, it may have been regarded as the navel of the world. Nearby, between the Tribune of Orators and the Temple of Saturn there are the broken remains of the *Milliarium*

aureum (Golden Mile Stone) erected by Augustus at the Via Sacra, which served to indicate the starting point of all the roads of the Empire and bore in letters of gold inscriptions of the distances between the principal cities and the capital.

It is hard to part from these columns and carvings, the remains of temple, governmental and representational buildings. On some of them it is possible to detect that gradual coarsening of the arts towards the close of the Empire. Difficult, too, to take leave of the colossal Basilica of Constantine, the vaults of which suggest an Eastern touch, something of the spirit of despotic sultans. It is pleasant to linger over inscriptions in that incisive Roman lettering which seems

117

THE TEMPLE OF SATURN
*on the northern edge of the Forum
Romanum, founded in 498 B.C. and
restored in 25 B.C. was the most
venerated sanctuary of Republican
Rome; eight Ionic granite columns
remain.*

ideally suited to preserve across the ages words cut into stone. There is the round Temple of Romulus with its green bronze door guarded by red pillars; the ancient lock can still be used today. We may be amused to see those old tablets of stone inlaid with chequered game boards similar to those often found on the parapets of cloisters which were used by the monks in their leisure hours. The virginal grace of the temple of Vesta adds an element of charm and gaiety to the gloomy atmosphere of the Forum. What it was like is clearly conveyed by the excavated remains of the House of the Vestal Virgins which up to the tenth century was occupied by members of the imperial and afterwards of the papal court. One imagines the original

Page 121

THE PANTHEON, dedicated to the seven planetary deities was erected in 27 B.C. by Marcus Agrippa, the son-in-law of Augustus. The actual building in its present form, however, is a reconstruction of Hadrian which has nothing in common with the old and smaller monument. Restored by Septimius Severus and Caracalla, closed and abandoned under the first Christian Emperors, pillaged by the Barbarians, the Pantheon was consecrated as a Christian church in 609 A.D. The special effect of the interior is due to the great cupola (142 ft in diameter) with five rows of lacunary which grow progressively smaller as they near the central and only opening (28 ft in diameter), the only source of light.

Page 122/123

THE ROMAN FORUM, centre of the economic and religious life of ancient Rome, was systematically excavated only in the 19th century. For centuries after the Forum was abandoned, it was overgrown with grass, it became pasture ground for cattle and was known as the Campo Vaccino.

Page 124

EQUESTRIAN STATUE OF THE EMPEROR MARCUS AURELIUS, the only remaining equestrian statue of the Roman Emperors, still bears traces of ancient gilding. The base of the bronze statue was executed after drawings by Michelangelo who also designed and built the new Piazza del Campidoglio.

Page 125

THE COLUMBARIUM, near the Scipio tomb between Porta San Sebastiano and Porta Latina, still within the area of the Aurelian wall, is typical of a pagan burial place of the 1st century B.C. The name "pigeon-house" for this kind of building with tiers of niches for the reception of cinerary urns was inspired by its resemblance to a dove cote. The Columbarium of Pomponio Hylas here illustrated was discovered only in 1830.

Page 126/127

THE COLOSSEUM or Flavian Amphitheatre, begun by Vespasian in 72 A.D. and finished by Titus in 80 A.D., is the largest monument of ancient Rome. Each of the four storeys of this immense buildung, 159 ft high, was comprised of 80 arches. The arena measured 249 ft by 150 ft. The exterior dimensions are: length 186 yards, breadth 170 yards, circumference 773 yards. The Circus was used for gladiatorial combats, but modern historians have disputed the old belief that St Ignatius of Antioch and other Christians were martyred in the arena. By the 15th century the amphitheatre had become a quarry for building material; it was dedicated to the Passion of Jesus by Pope Benedict IV in 1741.

Page 128

THE MAMERTINE PRISON, used as a dungeon for criminals and captives awaiting execution, was said to have been built by Servius Tullius in 387 B.C., though the name may have derived from *tullus* or *tullius,* which means a source of water. According to the Christian tradition St Peter was imprisoned here. A spring of water is shown in the building, called San Pietro in Carcere since the 16th century, which is supposed to have flowed forth at the bidding of the Saint so that he might baptize his gaolers.

Page 129

THREE COLUMNS REMAIN OF THE TEMPLE OF CASTOR AND POLLUX and have become the most characteristic features of the Roman Forum. The Temple was built in 484 B.C. by Aulus Postumius to commemorate the miraculous appearance of the Dioscuri, which secured the Roman victory over the Tarquins and Latins at the battle of Lake Regillus.

Page 130

SANTA MARIA MAGGIORE, fourth among the Patriarchal basilicas, is the largest of the Roman churches dedicated to the Virgin Mary. The first church was rebuilt by Sixtus III in 432–40 A.D. and further enlarged in the 12th, 13th and 17th centuries. The vast and magnificent interior, 279 ft long, which still preserves the basilican form is characterized by the gilded coffered ceiling attributed to Giuliano San Gallo (1445–1516) and by 36 antique marble columns and 4 columns in granite supporting an architrave adorned with mosaics.

Page 131

THE CORONATION OF THE VIRGIN in the apse of Santa Maria Maggiore is a masterwork of the Franciscan Friar and painter Jacopo Torriti (1292–1295). It commemorates the affirmation proclaimed at the Council of Ephesus in 431 of the title "Theotokos", mother of God.

Page 132

THE LACUS JUTURNAE on the Forum Romanum. This was the spring of the goddess Juturna at which Castor and Pollux were said to have watered their horses after the battle of Lake Regillus in 496 B.C.

VENI
ELEC
TAMÉ
ETPO

NÃM
TÉTH
RONÚ
OBV

MARIA·VIRGO·ASSVPTA·E·AD·ETHEREV·THALAMV·INQVO·REX·REGV·STELLATO·SEDET·SOLIO·+
EXALTATA·EST·SANCTA·DEI·GENITRIX·SVPER·CHOROS·ANGELORVO·AD·CELESTIA·REGNA·

inhabitants to have been a community, half religious half secular, of charming noble women devoted to good works. They were not allowed to use any kind of water except rain water because it came from heaven and was considered pure; the rain was collected in three cisterns in a rectangular courtyard formed by pillars. The basins have been restored and are filled with water and surrounded by roses.

The temples of Faustina and Romulus (not the founder of Rome but the son of an emperor who lived toward the end of the pagan era) have been turned into churches. The library of the Temple of Augustus became the church of Santa Maria Antiqua, which was destroyed by an earthquake in the early Middle Ages and is now a ruin in the midst of pre-Christian ruins, the subject also of many legends and stories. For some time the church was under the care of Greek monks and it was then that the magnificent wall paintings originated; in places there are even two or three layers of them. The severe solemnity of the pictures has been subdued by decay in some places but in others the colours have retained a marvellous freshness, as in the crucifixion scene depicting Christ in a sleeveless blue tunic with gold trimmings.

Santa Maria Antiqua is situated on a slope of the Palatine Hill. This area had earlier on developed as an exclusive residential district; Cicero, too, had a house there and Augustus who was born there enhanced it as an area for imperial representational functions. His successors followed in his footsteps, and hence we find there the palaces of Tiberius, of the Flavians, and of Septimius Severus. Even Theodoric, the Gothic king, had his residence on the Palatine. In time temples were added to the residential and official buildings of the court; the Temple of the Magna Mater, the Phrygian goddess of the powers of nature, was already built after the Second Punic War and serves as first evidence of the intrusion of Oriental cults which henceforth throughout five centuries gradually transformed the religion and cults of ancient Rome. When the birthplace of Augustus was struck by lightning, this was regarded as a sign that his patron god Apollo wished to take up residence there. Augustus thus built a temple, to the south-west of the later Colosseum site of a size and splendour unknown hitherto in Republican Rome. Julian the Apostate, in the romantic aftermath of the Pagan era, restored it once more to the worship of Apollo. Julian died far away in the East; and in the night of his death a fire destroyed the temple, the massive marble blocks, the first ones ever to be seen in Rome, were burned to lime, and traces of the formidable shrine are today recognizable only by well-trained eyes.

About the middle of the sixteenth century Cardinal Farnese's nephew laid out the gardens named after him. There are thus three particular features which determine the Palatine scenery: ancient princely gardens, ruins, a wooded park with exuberant natural growth. In addition there are the two churches on the upper part of the eastern slope, the garden between them, and, everywhere about the hill prospects opening out on the city, the Forum, the Colosseum, the distant tomb of Caecilia Metella and the Alban Hills. Oak and laurel trees, pines and cypresses, grave, unchangeable and ever-green, predominate. In such surroundings one may well meditate upon the traces of bygone glory. One wanders through the long underground passage, descends to the stadium and

THE BASILICA
OF CONSTANTINE
*or of Maxentius, begun by the latter
in 306–312 and completed by
Constantine, is typical of the Roman
hall of justice.*

strolls through the remains of the palace of Severus and its baths. One admires the bold architecture of the state apartments, especially the throne room, which exceeded even the width of the central nave of St Peter's by thirty feet, and one can look for the spot where the Emperor sat as justice. Of all the Palatine buildings one has a peculiar individual character. It is

the House of Livia, the first Empress in history who lived there with her first husband and there gave birth to Tiberius. Divorced and married to Augustus, whose life, honours and concerns she shared, she outlived him by a decade and a half spending these years in her former house. It is of moderate dimensions, a cross between an elegant villa and a small country mansion.

THE TEMPLE OF
ANTONINUS AND FAUSTINA
was dedicated by the Senate in
141 A.D. to the memory of the
Empress Faustina and, after his
death in 161 A.D., to her husband
Antoninus Pius. It was converted into
the church of San Lorenzo in
Miranda in the 11th century.

There are murals depicting scenes from everyday life or drawn from mythology in colours that still seem remarkably fresh.

Nero too, initially resided on the Palatine, but the thought of having to live in rooms built by his pre-decessors appears to have been intolerable to his pathological self-esteem. He was not satisfied even by what he had himself built on the Palatine. But the fire of Rome then offered him the opportunity of realizing his megalomaniac dreams. So the Golden

THE COLOSSEUM
*was built by the Emperors Vespasian
and Titus between 72 and 80 A.D.
as the amphitheatre of the Flavians.
This mightiest of buildings of ancient
Rome could accommodate
50,000 spectators.*

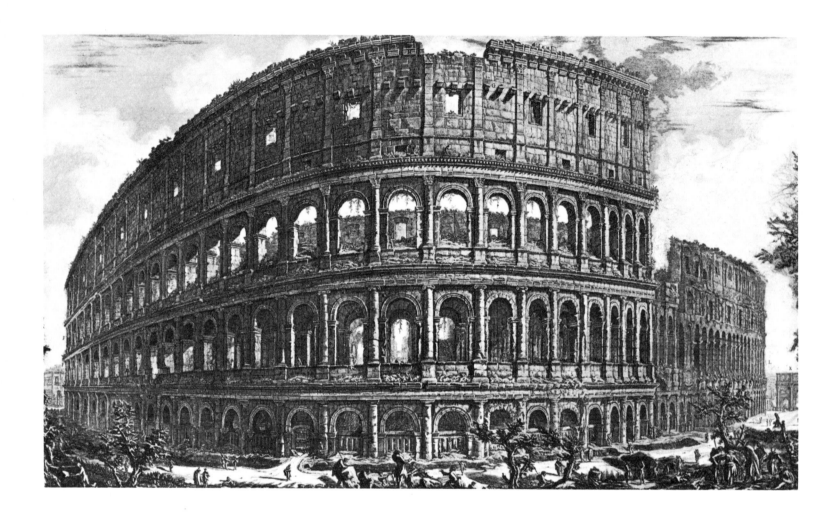

House was built, the ruins of which have come to light under the baths of Trajan. It was not just a palace, it was a whole complex of residential buildings, parks, zoos and all kinds of luxurious additions which extended from the Palatine to the Coelian and the Esquiline and across the low ground between the hills with parts of the Forum included. There is a certain analogy, though on a smaller scale, with the building mania exhibited by the mad King Ludwig II of Bavaria or by Hitler and Mussolini, though in their

case with additional shabbiness and lack of taste. Anxious to obliterate the memory of Nero, his successors destroyed the Golden House or incorporated parts of it in their own buildings, baths, temples and in the Colosseum. This erasion of memories, understandable though it is in the case of Nero, became customary in the era of the Caesars. After Caracalla had murdered his brother and co-regent Geta, he had his portrait chiselled out from the sculptures of the Arch of the Money Changers and erased his name from the

136

THE CHURCH OF
SANTI GIOVANNI E PAOLO
*was built above the house of these two
saints martyred under Julian the
Apostate in the 4th century.*

triumphal arch which the two brothers had erected in their own honour, but also in their father's, Septimius Severus. Parts of the Golden House were torn down, partly buried under artificial mounts. Of the three thousand six hundred rooms which, according to tradition – no doubt with the usual exaggeration – are supposed to have existed, some are roofless and were filled in with earth and stones. The cost of the building had shaken the financial structure of the State and its dismantling, too, must have been expensive enough. One walks through courtyards, gardens and rooms without roofs. A row of apartments was built in curved form so that they received the sunlight throughout the winter. Light entered through alabaster windows. Some of the apartments used by Nero himself, for example his own and Poppaea's bedrooms, are

clearly recognizable. The Emperor never sat at table with his guests, but took his meals apart in a kind of side room in chapel form whence he could observe them, for it was not fitting for a god to eat with mortals. The dining table was contained in a water basin and rose up driven by a hydraulic device; it was lowered again after the meal. One is also shown the cupola of the dining room which opened up to allow some exotic essence to be sprayed down, but also sometimes, used for that legendary shower of roses to suffocate those who had fallen into disgrace after they had been sumptuously entertained.

Michelangelo and Raphael were fascinated by the ruins. We are told that Raphael climbed about the half-buried vaults sketching the ornaments of the murals by candle light. Many of them can be recognized in the Loggias of the Vatican or in the Farnesina. With the charred end of his candle Raphael wrote his own signature on one of the walls. Other discoveries too were made in the Golden House: the Laocoon Group, the Apollo Belvedere and the Farnese Hercules were unearthed in the Temple interior.

The Colosseum, that imposing creation of the Flavian dynasty, indirectly owes its name to Nero, for a giant statue of himself, called the colossus, which depicted him as the god of the sun crowned by its rays, was put up in the courtyard of the Golden House. His successors, in destroying the palace left it intact. Presumably, and for understandable reasons, they hesitated to destroy a monument which expressed so powerful an idea: man raised to divine status as emperor. Under Hadrian the statue, 108 feet tall, was set up on a site between the Colosseum and the Temple of Venus and Roma. With that typical human

disposition for turning relative appearances into absolute ones, the proverbial saying came about that Rome would last as long as the Colossus; if it fell, Rome too would fall, and the world with it. In the early Middle Ages – one doesn't even know when – it fell indeed, but Rome and the world continued to exist.

The Colosseum, too, has outlasted the ages, a work of man that defies comparison with anything else. Only one third of it stands, a wreath of walls deprived of its leaves, but this fragment forms a whole, as a mountain does, though, from a geological point of view, it would appear to be but the last remnant of a former range of mountains. Its stones and pillars have been used for innumerable Roman buildings of later times; its architectural ideas have inspired buildings throughout the Western world. Its historical course is unique. It was theatre, arena for gladiators, site of martyrdoms, place of pilgrimage, fortress, quarry, ruin; as a sort of myth it has finally entered the consciousness of Western man as one of his great symbols.

The hilly regions to the south, around the Aventine and Coelian, were densely populated areas in ancient times, with their tall tenement buildings of the plebeian quarter. Both these summits became deserted later and in the Middle Ages there were only some solitary churches, monasteries and gardens; a few fortifications existed such as one built by the Emperor Otto III next to the monastery of Sant'Alessio. But its actual development began only in this century, and even in the very midst of modern urban growth something remains of the old monastic peace. Many houses are surrounded by gardens, there are no tramways, no cafes and hardly any shops. The churches, for the most part close to one another, date back to the early Middle Ages or the times of the Barbarian invasions. Santa Sabina with the open-work roofing of an early Christian basilica, is the cradle of the Dominican Order. An orange tree in the garden, planted by its founder, is somehow symbolic of the Aventine's peaceful atmosphere. According to an old tradition, St Peter is supposed to have lived in Santa Prisca. There is a beautiful view from this simple church built upon ancient foundations. You look at the Lower Aventine and the church of San Saba with its many invaluable early Christian treasures. Like Santo Stefano, it belongs to the German College. Its columned loggia of the upper storey is surrounded by green trees, and it seems to rise up against the sky like a picture of the early Renaissance on a golden background.

The south and south-east of Rome, particularly the Aventine, Coelian and Esquiline areas, clearly convey the natural rise of religious ritual from the everyday life of the ancient world. At first it was the custom for a Christian who owned a large enough house, to set aside a room for communal worship with his fellow-Christians. Later rebuilding and building extensions became necessary, for instance, to provide accommodations for priests and deacons. It was not until quite late that churches proper were built. In this way our church buildings have developed from Roman private houses like the temples of the pagan era derived from the ancient peasant houses. It happened not infrequently that a house became the property of a community by way of a legacy or donation and that parts of it were turned into an embryonic church. Or that a martyr's house was transformed into a church, like San Giovanni e Paolo, the parental home of two brothers, court officials, who, under Julian the Apostate, suffered martyrdom and found their eternal rest in their own home. Again, a Christian might hand over his father's house to be used as a monastery which he himself joined, as in the case of Gregory the Great.

Accounts such as these may invest some of the early Christian churches with their warm and vital atmosphere; something of the spirit of the original inhabitants seems to live on in them. Figures come to life again such as the Roman senator Pudens, baptized by the apostles; his daughters Pudentiana and Praxedis; his sons Novatus and Timotheus. The great Pope Gregory's mother Silvia had a house on the Aventine which later became the monastery of San Saba. The Pope's own room and chair can be seen as well as the long stone table at which twelve poor men were admitted daily to be fed. The inscription carved into the stone reads: "Twelve of the poor were entertained here by Gregory and an angel joined them as the thirteenth."

THE STREETS AND SQUARES OF ROME

A mere glimpse is often enough to discover how some of Rome's streets came into being. One, for instance, in the old part of the city traces the curved line of an ancient amphitheatre that is no longer there, another runs through the long vale between two parallel heights. Others are evidently thoroughfares, driven through a maze of narrow medieval streets and they may indicate the forceful intervention of one or another among the papal reformers of the city. The long straight Corso reminds us by its name of the horse races (the horses, by the way, ran riderless) that at one time were staged there during the Carnival. It is the old military highway leading north which, outside the city, changes its name to Via Flaminia and it is the main artery of the traffic in modern Rome. Though usually hectically alive, there are times of the day – in the late morning and at certain hours in the afternoon – when it appears mysteriously deserted and silent. On a house at the northern end there is a plaque recording that "Volfgango Goethe lived here", opposite the Palazzo Rondanini which for centuries housed Michelangelo's unfinished Pietà. How Goethe fared in this house, indeed in Rome, this "university and capital of the world", he tells us repeatedly.

"I count a second birthday, a true rebirth of the day when I entered Rome . . . Where, for the first time in my life, I was absolutely happy . . . Indeed, I can say that only in Rome I felt what man actually is. Such heights, such happiness of feeling, I attained never again; indeed, compared to my state of mind in Rome, I have never been able later to recapture joyfulness . . . Rome is a world . . . Its tremendous impact acts upon us quite calmly while we rush to and fro . . . Every day reveals something new and remarkable, every day presents new, great and amazing pictures and a whole which one may long think and dream about yet never capture with the imagination. One would need to write in a thousand styles; what is the use of a single pen!"

The Corso links Piazza del Popolo with Piazza Venezia, the approach to the Capitol and the Forum Romanum – thus with the very heart of the city.

Old pictures still suggest the glorious unity of the Piazza Venezia before the Victor Emanuel Monument was erected. The square owes its name and fame to the Palazzo Venezia. No other Italian State was so proudly represented in Rome as the Republic of Venice, which was once the hub not only of the maritime but also of the artistic power of the Italian north-east. The palace originated from the church of San Marco, which in its turn had been a palace in the late classical era. Near the church arose a fortified tower used as a Cardinal's dwelling which Cardinal Pietro Barbo, later Pope Paul II, a Venetian, about the middle of the fifteenth century enlarged into a building of a completely new architectural type. The fortress effect of the old building was retained but fused now with a magnificent, noble type of palace unknown in medieval Rome. The bold experiment of returning to the architectural forms of antiquity, to pillars, for instance, supported by pilasters, as in the Theatre of Marcellus or in the Colosseum, produced the stupendous though unfinished two-storeyed columned courtyard. The Palazzo Venezia marks the transition from the warring Roman Middle Ages to the courtly and festive style of the Renaissance. It was a marriage of fortress and mansion, of defensive and representational features. As papal property the palace served as summer residence and stronghold on the boundary of the old city. Later on it was acquired by Venice and so passed to the Habsburg Empire. After the First World War the Italian kingdom became the new owner and Mussolini made it the centre of the Fascist State. It comprises many marvelous features, above all the Palazzetto, a cloistered fairy garden, which was moved westward some decades ago though mercifully without impairing its beauty, and many large rooms for centuries have served as models for some of Europe's great ceremonial halls.

The Piazza del Popolo derives ist name from the church of the Augustinian Fathers Santa Maria del Popolo, next to the Porta del Popolo. Its name has been explained as indicating a church built by the people. It has also been suggested that the name comes from a grove of poplar trees and a church dedicated to Our Lady of the Poplars. A tree was actually known as a landmark in this formerly deserted area, but it was not a poplar but a walnut tree. The place was said to be haunted by the ghosts from the graves of the Domitian family, especially Nero's, nearby. Pope Paschal II had the tree finally cut down and the evil spirits, so the story goes, rushed out of the branches like a pack of wild cats. Paschal had a chapel built which was replaced by a church in the late Middle Ages. Other accounts refer to an oak tree; the old tradition about the poplars is the one I would prefer, in order once and for all to put an end to the dispute among the experts. Only a minor part of the Augustinian monastery, in which Luther lived as an Augustinian monk, has been preserved since the Sack of Rome by the mercenaries of Charles V. Luther is believed to have preached in the church. It contains many superb paintings and sculptures; few of the great names in the history of Italian art are missing.

The Piazza del Popolo today gives no indication of having been haunted. Since the beginning of the last century the square has been variously adorned, endowed with a somewhat light-hearted and free symmetry, the living element of variety being provided by the wall, covered with green foliage, of the Pincio on the eastern side of the square. Two fountains face one another at the intersecting points of the two semicircles of stone surrounding the round Piazza, and the recumbent sphinxes have their affinity with the high obelisk surrounded by lions in the centre. It originated in the twelfth or thirteenth century B.C. and was put up in the Circus Maximus by Augustus after the conquest of Egypt.

Time and again we are reminded of the importance which the encounter with Egypt had for the ancient

THE THEATRE
OF MARCELLUS,
*begun by Julius Caesar, completed by
Augustus in 13 B.C. and dedicated to
the son of his sister Octavia. In the
16th century the remains were
incorporated in the palace of the
Savelli which later passed to the
Orsini.*

Roman world. Egypt came into fashion in Rome as chinoiserie did in eighteenth-century Europe. For Roman grandees at the end of the classical age it was the thing to do to have colossal Egyptian antiquities brought back and put up in the city. The Emperor Hadrian, in particular, seems to have been fascinated by Egypt as a land of ancient and mysterious wisdom.

Egyptian deities were taken over by Roman religion, Egyptian hieroglyphs, patterns and ornaments influenced the Roman arts. The fact that all of us in the Western world are so familiar from childhood on with pyramids, obelisks and sphinxes is largely due to the way they have indirectly travelled via Rome. Three important roads radiate southwards from this obelisk,

143

THE PIAZZA DEL POPOLO
*with the Flaminian Obelisk,
73 ft high, and the churches of Santa
Maria in Montesanto (left) and
Santa Maria dei Miracoli (right),
both executed, after designs of Carlo
Rainaldi (1611–1691), by Bernini
and Carlo Fontana (1634–1714).*

the central one being the Corso, to the left the Via del Babuino leading to the Spanish Steps and to the right the Via Ripetta, called after the bank of the river, which continues under different names until it eventually disappears somewhat infamously in the maze of little streets between the Piazza Navona and the Pantheon. Where the Corso leaves the Piazza there are two Baroque churches of Our Lady designed to match each other, on either side.

Equalling the Corso in importance is the Via Sistina named after Sixtus V, who was largely responsible for the city's eastward expansion. It also begins at an

obelisk, that of Santa Trinità dei Monti which, once used to stand in the Gardens of Sallust. Changing its name several times it runs from north-west to south-east up and downhill across the Quirinal, Viminal and Esquiline. One of its small marvels is the Piazza delle Quattro Fontane where an ordinary cross-road has been turned into an enclosed space in octagonal shape without any damage having been done to its initial character as a street junction. Each of the four buildings had its corner cut off so that the fountains could be placed against the newly created facades. Four river deities in recumbent, relaxed position dispense the water of these fountains. The German archaeologist J. Winckelmann (1717–1768), to whom so much is owing of the discovery and preservation of Roman antiquities, lived opposite the little church of San Carlino, the first work of Borromini. The facade seems anxious to avoid horizontal straight lines. Everything appears to move in curves and waves and gives an almost musical and melodious impression. Only the vertical lines, represented by columns, rise straight up. There is a marvellous harmony in this proportion of lines, disproving the superficial opinion that only Gothic arches and clustered pillars can express man's longing for heaven. This facade indeed seems to symbolize the cosmic unity as it were of heaven and earth in a living system of relationships. In the interior elliptical forms are expressed in most imaginative and original fashion while all concessions to colour effect have been resisted. The adjoining two-storeyed courtyard of columns takes up the old idea of cloisters, but in its rectangular form expands upwards only and not in breadth. As though unwilling to be outdone by his rival, the ageing Bernini built another church,

Sant'Andrea al Quirinale nearby, also on an elliptic ground plan, a cupola covered space of pure harmony, decorated in reddish, gold and grey.

The street now reaches its highest point, the Esquiline and Santa Maria Maggiore, visible from afar by its two domes and the slender bell tower. This campanile is considered to be the highest in the city and the pointed roof that is its continuation exemplifies a type of building rare in Rome. Approaching it we are faced by another obelisk and behind it the oldest and largest of Roman Marian churches. The front and rear facades are equally splendidly solemn, indeed, at the rear there is a graceful flight of steps over which rises the Tribuna, a particular embellishment.

The history of Santa Maria Maggiore which covers fifteen centuries is no less varied than that of St Peter's, with great names to mark all its stages. Indeed, the Church has undergone more alterations than St Peter's if not such profound ones and hence, more than St Peter's it has retained something of the spirit of the early Church and its close links with antiquity. This seems to be a characteristic of the site. With the Campo Marzio reflecting the medieval and the Baroque papal city, the Capitol and the Palatine and their surroundings representing ancient Rome, the Coelian, Aventine, Viminale and Esquiline form that region in which early Roman Christianity is still closest to us today. This spirit of Christian antiquity is expressed, in defiance of all later alterations and additions, in the edifice itself, above all in the nave with its 36 ionic columns of white marble but also by its ornamentation. There is the ancient porphyry urn with its relics under the high altar, there are the mosaics on the triumphal arch above the entablature which in the antique manner depict scenes from the Old and New Testament. In the apse we have the new art of Jacopo Torriti whose style, while forming part of a progressive development in the thirteenth century, is very much in the Byzantine tradition and yet strongly individualistic. But newer epochs have also contributed to the decoration of Santa Maria Maggiore.

No other Roman church can display a feeling of such elegance and splendour. The first gold to be brought from the newly discovered Americas glistens across its expanse and when there is sunlight it is reflected from the floor. It is part of the most splendid features of the Renaissance that henceforth in Roman churches the precious marble decorations of the

floor often find harmonious response in the ceiling ornamentation.

Strolling about in the neighbourhood of Santa Maria Maggiore and leaving our straight road for a while, we are quite suddenly transported back into apostolic times, into the era in which, according to an ancient tradition of the Church, the blood of Christ still had its purple colouring. Santa Pudenziana is considered to be the oldest church in Rome. Its traditions are of apostolic origins and it looks as though the first Roman bishops of the pre-Constantine Epoch might well have resided there. Of a later date is the sister church Santa Prassede, insignificant, even hardly noticeable from the outside because it is enveloped by houses near it, as though humbly expressing the poverty of the early Church; in the interior, however, it reveals magnificent treasures. The mosaics on the triumphal arch and the apse and still more those in the chapel, formerly known

Page 149

THE ELEPHANT OBELISK on the Piazza della Minerva, one of
the most charming among Roman monuments, was made
by Ercole Ferrata (1610–1685) according to a plan by
Bernini (1667). The obelisk of the 4th century B.C. was
taken from a Temple of Isis which formerly stood nearby.

Page 150/151

THE FAME OF ROME as the capital of the Christian world was
powerfully underlined in our time by the Second Vatican
Council. Hundreds of thousands filled St Peter's Square
when Pope Paul VI impartet the blessing "urbi et orbi" at
the final session on December 8th 1965.

Page 152

ROMAN TOMB on the Via Appia.

as the "Garden of Paradise", gleaming in ancient dark gold exude the fervent transcendent spirit of apocalyptic and eschatological religiosity. These mosaics may well carry the observer back beyond the Carolingian Age of their origin to that period of Christian antiquity to which the wonderful mosaics in the apse of Santa Pudenziana belong. It was in Santa Prassede, incidentally, "which ever was the church for peace", that Browning's bishop ordered his tomb.

Close to the ancient portal of Santa Prassede, now generally kept locked, is the tower-like house in which lived the painter Domenichino, "little Dominic" of Bologna, whose works are so frequently encountered in Rome. According to the inscription of the memorial plaque it is an oasis of peace in a world of envy and strife. Goethe greatly admired Domenichino. Having seen his frescoes of the Apostles and Evangelists, he wrote that he could hardly describe his joy on that day; it was too much for months, let alone a single day. I share this admiration to a certain extent, but not fully, for I have misgivings about the speed with which Domenichino seems to surrender to the influence of any master once he has become visibly famous, making their style his own by almost plagiarizing them, regardless of whether it be Carracci, Raphael, Michelangelo, Correggio or his fellow-countryman Guido Reni. Almost everyone of his brilliant works has its models, and scarcely one is free from "borrowings". One has to admit this even when considering the extent to which throughout the whole of Roman art that time all sorts of movements reverberate, as started by the great creative masters, and how after Michelangelo God the Father hovering over the clouds, Prophets and Sibyls recur in countless variations until they gradually pale into insignificance. It will always remain odd and instructive how easily the great Goethe, having once turned against the original minds of the German Storm and Stress period, came himself to appreciate and eclectic and academic type of virtuosity. Domenichino, who arrived in Rome in 1602, was popular with his patrons and public, but met with opposition from his fellow-artists. He suffered from depression and his weak character inclined him to extreme touchiness so that an atmosphere of intrigue and strife formed around him both in Rome and Naples. One has not got much confidence that the force of peace mentioned in the inscription at his house was very effective in the life of this gifted man so much at variance with himself and others.

Beyond the Basilica of Santa Maria Maggiore our street continues under the name of Via Carlo Alberto. The long rectangular Piazza Vittorio with its palm trees is surrounded by stalls; here one of the jolliest and most tumultuous and colourful of Roman street markets has developed. There may be a puppet show in the centre which will bring back pleasant childhood memories. The only other market to be compared with this one on the south-east slopes of the Esquiline is the Campo di Fiori, the old execution site, where Giordano Bruno was burned to death.

These two markets might stand as examples of the many other Roman markets and "bancarelle" (street stalls). They are all reminiscent of country fairs. There are books, antiques, junk, bundles of old rusty keys – heaven only knows what locks they are supposed to fit –, there is poultry (usually alive), chickens, ducks, turkeys, and also a variety of singing birds, meat, flowers, fruit, vegetables, cheese, mussels, snails, mushrooms, fish, in all sizes and colours often displayed on large green leaves, sometimes arranged in star shapes. There are little fish sparkling like polished pewter. And all this in quantities which make the inexperienced foreigner wonder how they can ever be sold. Among the crowd of buyers and onlookers, among those who would inspect everything carefully and bargain noisily, women are by no means in the majority. Often one will see the typical Roman, head of a lower middle-class family, buying something that takes his fancy, and having it wrapped up in newspaper to take home to his wife to cook, saying "Here you are, fry me this fish".

You can also buy crockery, glassware, musical instruments, records, toilet articles, bicycles, second-hand shoes, coats, material, old an new clothes. The Roman people and especially those living in the country prefer to do their shopping in street markets. They feel shy in the big shops where they are served by smart salesmen with their persuasive talk. They are afraid, too, of being cheated in some way and having to pay also for what seems to them the luxuriously furnished store. In the markets they are among themselves, safe, under the open sky. There are many small shop-keepers who even in winter make do without a shop door, using merely the shutters at night. They know very well that the customers used to open air business are put off by a door; the door of a shop closing gives them the impression of being trapped.

The street vendors shout to sell their goods, some play gramophone records or mouth organs, fowls cackle, geese gaggle, but there is something to be said for the fish, for they at least, if not their vendors, are unable to join in the general hullabaloo. Over one of the stalls selling khakis, an orange coloured juicy fruit, two long slightly bowed ox horns pointing upwards have been fixed to the rods; they are to avert the evil eye, the dreaded *malocchio*. In the autumn or winter, an open fire burns cheerfully here and there among the crowds, with broken fruit boxes, vegetable baskets, twings and newspapers serving as fuel. No policeman will object, for what could be more natural, and therefore permissible than for a salesman working in the open air to light a fire when he feels cold? The street cleaners too, representatives of municipal authority though they may be, act no differently; they make short shrift by burning all the rubbish on the spot and remove simply what they cannot burn. Nor is there any hesitation to put brightly burning braziers in the street till the wood has become charcoal to be used for heating and cooking, for it is not the burning, but the continuous glow that produces the required heat. Thus the carpenter will put outside his door a brazier with a pot of glue on the boil. Beyond the market, our street in the form of a wide and spacious boulevard, leads straight towards the white porch of Santa Croce in Gerusalemme with its reddish grey campanile to the right among trees, outlined against the blue haze of the Alban hills. Before we get there the street traverses over the arches of the Claudian aqueducts which, farther on cross the garden of the Villa Wolkonsky; to the left visible from behind the walls, is the light grey portal of the Porta Maggiore.

The church of Santa Croce will probably appeal to the devout rather than to the art lover. The interior is gloomy and lacks warmth, the outside suffers from the neighbouring facade of the Lateran which dwarfs it.

At the portal of Santa Croce ends the street that

brought us all the way from Trinità dei Monti. The square in front of the church is liked with the Lateran area by a wide street running south-westwards. We are now facing San Giovanni. Its heavy dimensions have been happily harmonized by its vertical lines. The columns and pillars rising in two storeys are continued on top of the roof by statues of the Fathers of the Church holding their croziers; the whole group led by the central figure of Christ with the cross.

The two extreme types among the Roman piazzas, according to which all others can be classified, are St Peter's Square and the Lateran Square or Squares, since there are three merging into one. The Piazza San Pietro is the result of a grandiose design, the Piazza San Giovanni in Laterano the result of haphazard development. It is asymmetrical, bustling with activity, worn out by life. Its gardens seem almost neglected, but they are used all day long by the people and cannot

155

PIAZZA DI SAN GIOVANNI
IN LATERANO
with the Lateran Palace and the
octagonal Battistero di San Giovanni
(right).

be kept in better condition. The Piazza serves as a highly frequented, noisy thoroughfare, while St Peter's has no other goal than itself. There are large crowds on the Piazza Laterano; it is teaming with tramways, cars, children, street vendors hawking fruit, bowls of gold-fish that glisten in the bright sunshine. St Peter's Square is enormous, solemn, empty even when crowds are gathered there. It is untouched by everyday life and seems to absorb all noise. There are green trees in the Lateran Square whereas in St Peter's Square there is no green at all. All nature is strictly subject to the spirit of the place. Everything is governed by the majestic nakedness of fashioned stone, as though in emphasis of the meaning of Peter, *petra,* rock. The

white gushing waters of the two fountains are the only evidence here of living nature.

For a thousand years the Lateran had the significance which, for the last five hundred years, has been accorded to the Vatican. The Lateran originally belonged to a family of that name, later became the property of the emperors and was then bestowed by Constantine on the Roman bishopric. All that remains of the old palace lies underground, and there is also an old part of the building that now houses the Scala Santa. During the Middle Ages restorations and extensions were carried out on the palace and the basilica next to it founded by Constantine, but after the great fire of 1308 the ruin could no longer be averted, particularly since, a year later, the papacy moved to Avignon. This event marks the beginning of an epoch of Roman decline which surpassed all the catastrophic effects of the Barbarian invasion and of those dark ages from the death of Charlemagne to the rise of the Ottonian German Empire. The city grew deserted and became impoverished, continual fighting coincided with natural disasters such as the earthquake of 1345 and the Black Death of 1348. The population, said to have numbered about a million in imperial times – a number never reached again until this century – was probably reduced to some twenty thousand, mostly brigands, beggars, and rascals preying on pilgrims. The great buildings decayed, not infrequently packs of wolves penetrated the city. In an old report which the Cathedral Chapter of St Peter's submitted to the Holy See, it was stated the faithful no longer ventured as far as St Peter's church because they were afraid of being killed on the way by collapsing buildings.

Even the return of the Pope to Rome brought no immediate change except a gradual preparation for a more prosperous future. In fact it was not until the fifteenth century that there were signs of prosperity again, under rulers such as Martin V, a member of the Colonna family, whose bronze memorial is in the enclosure in front of the Lateran Basilica's Confessio; and under Pope Nicholas V, one of the great patrons of the arts who is remembered by the chapel in the Vatican adorned by the frescoes of Fra Angelico.

It took Rome a long time to catch up with the progress made in those years by the Italian cities of the north. That Rome finally succeeded in raising itself from that abyss of its ruin is part of the miracles and at the same time of the decisive events of European history. Only one hundred and twenty-five years after the end of the Papal exile the most golden of Roman ages had become a fact. Although the works of repair on the Lateran Basilica had not completely ceased during the papal exile, the palace itself remained in ruins until in the sixteenth century the energetic Pope Sixtus V embarked upon a new building, something which none of his predecessors had dared attempt. The Lateran remained papal property also after 1870 and up to the reconciliation between the Church and the Italian State. Today it is far less extensive than the medieval papal palace which must have been a formidable and fortified complex of church buildings, residences, offices, school and assembly rooms. It also embraced those buildings on the north-east side, which are now separated from the main part in which the Sacred Stairs are venerated and ascended by visitors on their knees. According to tradition this was the staircase leading up to the platform in front of Pilate's house in Jerusalem and would therefore have been used by the Saviour. It is uncertain whether it was brought to Rome on the initiative of the Empress Helena or shortly before the conquest of Jerusalem by the Saracens, or only during the crusades.

At the top of the stairs is the ancient private chapel of the pope, a room in the Gothic style, the Sancta Sanctorum, not accessible to the public, but visible from the outside. Its name derives from the large number of relics collected and kept there in pre-Carolingian times. Among these treasures is the famous Byzantine picture of Christ, painted on cypress wood which was brought to Rome in the eighth century, and, so the legend goes, in miraculous fashion. It is one of those paintings which, according to popular belief, was not made by human hands but is of heavenly origin. In medieval times the picture was covered with silver and only the face was left free. In the covering there is a little door concealing the feet which used to be opened on Easter morning, when Pope and Cardinals kissed the feet of the risen Lord.

On the eastern side of the building containing the Scala Santa and this chapel is a tall niche open to the outside with shining gold mosaics glittering in the sun, which is one of the unforgettable features of the Lateran. It was built by Pope Benedict XIV as an exact replica of a work of art dating back almost a thousand years in which some of the old parts have been incorporated, such as the mosaics of the western apse of the dining hall which Leo III had built in the Lateran Palace in honour of his guest the Emperor Charlemagne. This occasion is commemorated in the mosaic: the vault depicts the sending forth of the apostles and St Peter holding a long patriarchal cross in his hands stands at the right side of Christ. On the left wall we see Christ sitting on the throne giving the keys to Pope Silvester and the standard to the Emperor Constantine; on the right wall St Peter is shown bestowing the pallium, or according to a different version, a stole on Pope Leo III and the standard on Charlemagne. The significance is that the spiritual and the temporal power both spring from the same source, both having to serve in union and yet each in its own sphere, the eternal and temporal good of mankind.

The Lateran Basilica of San Giovanni also has a northern facade apart from the eastern one. It carries the two characteristic steeples and before it there is the tallest obelisk in Rome (105 ft high, 154 ft with pedestal). Three great names are connected with it: King Thotmes IV, who erected it at Thebes in Upper-Egypt fifteen centuries before Christ, the Emperor Constantius II, who placed it in the Circus Maximus, and Pope Sixtus V, who transferred it to its present position, the very same site where formerly the equestrian statue of Marcus Aurelius had stood.

When the basilica was rebuilt a great deal was destroyed inside, the loss of which is more painful to us than it could have been to the men of the Baroque age.

This is particularly true of the frescoes by the great painters of the early Renaissance, Gentile da Fabriano and Pisanello, who mark the beginning of a new epoch of Roman art. Borromini, who carried out the work of reconstruction on the middle of the seventeenth century, was certainly as anxious as his patron Pope Innocent X to preserve as much as possible. However, historical feeling and reverence for tradition were hardly the distinctive characteristics of the Baroque age, a time of dynamic and exuberant creativeness. It is only in epochs without a style of their own that the work of artistic salvage is felt to be necessary. Nevertheless, the interior has the majesty that is fitting for the cathedral church of the bishops of Rome. The Gothic canopy, the copies of the old apse mosaics of Jacopo Torriti, the magnificent wooden Renaissance ceiling, the floor given by Martin V, all these features link the present with the Basilicas long time-honoured and faithful past. The altar of the Blessed Sacrament protrudes powerfully from the wall of the left transept like an ancient golden temple; four antique pillars of gilded bronze stood in the original basilica. An ancient Roman poet said that the story of a single family suffices to illustrate the character of the whole human race; in the same sense we may see summarized and exemplified two thousand years of Roman history in the Lateran Basilica and in the Lateran Palace.

In the Middle Ages the largely ruined city at times consisted of various districts separated from one another by deserted areas, in which something of a special local attachment developed. Traces of this can still be found. The inhabitants of Trastevere in particular are regarded today as a group apart, not quite amalgamated with the Roman population as a whole. They speak a dialect of their own and are fond boasting of their descent from pure ancient Roman stock.

Trastevere is that part of the city which reflects most strongly the colourful, wild and energetic temperament of the South, sometimes reminiscent of Naples. Nowhere else in Rome does the washing seem to dangle and flutter so lustily from the tops of houses and across the street as in Trastevere. It is picturesque, noisy, and the Romans love it, though it may appear dirty to fussy foreigners. But then natural animal life just isn't clean and tidy, and has no complexes about cleanliness and order; with hygiene it rejects the triumph of reason over instinct. In the streets garbage is heaped high, a feeding ground for stray cats and dogs. There seem to be more dogs in Trastevere than in other parts, creatures of all imaginable colours, sizes and shapes, and experienced dog lovers would find it impossible to trace their descent. It may happen too that the stroller in Trastevere will be brought up short by a dead canary, a cleanly nibbled chop bone or empty corn cob that may suddenly land at his feet, thrown down from some window above and disturbing him abruptly in his thoughts. He should regard himself as fortunate that it missed him and be satisfied with the simple truth, that the most natural way to get rid of things which are a nuisance is to chuck them out of the window. Repeated walks in Trastevere will promote an understanding for this philosophy. Its natural and unsophisticated way of life is not the only lovable attraction of Trastevere. Situated between the river and the green Gianicolo, the ancient churches of Santa Maria in Trastevere, Santa Cecilia and San Crisogono, palaces of rural character, make Trastevere more than a charming locality and give it an air of relaxed and weather-beaten glory. Pope Giulius II linked Trastevere with the Borgo by a straight road, the Lungara. The Via della Lungara leaves from the Porta Settimiana in the south said to have been built Septimius Severus, and leads up to the sombre, unfinished Porta Santo Spirito in the north which was part of the Renaissance fortifications. It runs parallel with the Tiber, but without following its winding bed. In the northern part there are houses only on one side of the street, since the buildings opposite with their gardens had to make way for the regulating of the Tiber. With many older streets this street shares the live and contrasting coexistance of noble palaces and poorer living quarters.

At the very beginning stands the Palazzo Corsini, the gardens of which extend up to the Gianicolo. Here lived and died, surrounded by an odd set of scholars, musicians, intriguers and political dilettantes, Christina of Sweden, perhaps the most remarkable of all the Queens of Europe. The daughter of Gustavus Adolphus, she was received into the Catholic Church, a spirited, scholarly, vacillating and restless woman who was laid to her final rest under the marble floor of St Peter's. At the Papal Court she had often been an inconvenient and costly guest and her eccentricities amply served the Roman need for gossip. In her time this district enjoyed a fashionable, social and courtly splendour; there was a much frequented Corso, later transferred to the area of Porta Pia and finally to the Pincio, where it has lately died, but it was so much a part of Roman life that it is perhaps premature to write its obituary now. In the new Palazzo Corsini, built after Christina's death, Joseph Bonaparte, Napoleon's brother, took up residence in 1797 as minister, or, as we might say today, as leader of a fifth column. All the intrigues aimed at the overthrow of the papal government were centred on this palace. The French General Duphot lost his life as a victim of the conspiracies engineered there. The event provided an excuse for the occupation of the papal state by the French and a republican regime was founded. The eighty year old Pius VI was arrested and taken to northern Italy and France. What followed then and lasted up to the Congress of Vienna was a parallel to the papal exile in Avignon, also known as the Babylonian captivity of the Church.

Agostino Chigi the banker and patron of the arts, whose tomb in Santa Maria del Popolo was designed by Raphael, had a house and garden built opposite the Palazzo Corsini, also built, it is thought, by Raphael with the assistance of Baldassare Peruzzi. Later the property passed into the hands of the Farnese family and under the name of Farnesina it has become a place of bliss for everyone. The Farnesina was decorated by Raphael and his disciples, Peruzzi, Sodoma, Sebastiano del Piombo and Giulio Romano, the only painter of renown actually born in the city which was the foster mother of so many other artists. The whole edifice is a hymn of praise to the glories of the earth and all earthly powers and passions with heaven and the planets arched high above it, a heaven of the Ptolemaic tradition, of course, meaningfully filled with planetary deities and signs of the zodiac. The human, natural and harmonious character of the Italian people has rarely found such pure expression as it has here. The gaiety of this heaven of the gods so humanly conceived and painted in olympic blue, accords with the image which Renaissance men had of ancient mythology. We know that they saw but one side of this Janus-headed world, yet, how pleasant it is to enter into this aspect of creation which strikes us as being complete in itself. Even the gods seem to be subject to human nature in that world and this is no denigration of the gods but raises human nature to divine heights. In that world, passion seems to unite gods and men. All the gods celebrate the marriage of Cupid and Psyche and Hermes gives the cup of immortality to his suffering lover. Galathea and her followers ride the waves, ornate forms blossom in tropic exuberance; hundreds of figures half-divine and half-human animate creation and include the

Veduta del Palazzo Farnese

onlooker in their Olympic freedom. We become partakers of the magic joining with the gods at table and without incurring the guilt of sacrilege, we feel enriched and happy. Mock-windows show prospects of Rome as it was in Raphael's days. In the garden hall below, the painted architectural prospects seem to reach a climax of illusion. All this may not be the best of art, but here it has the accent of festive gaiety and fits perfectly into the atmosphere of the place.

Before the regulation of the river, the Farnesina Gardens extended down to the Tiber. If Michelangelo's wish had been fulfilled, there would have been a bridge across the river connecting the Farnesina and the Palazzo Farnese and thus joining brilliant gaiety with proud grandeur. But Michelangelo died and the second courtyard of the Palazzo Farnese was never built. Today, therefore, the Palazzo does not border on the river, but on the Via Giulia, that lovely straight road which

THE PALAZZO ODESCALCHI
*on the Via del Corso in the
Florentine style of the 15th century –
one of the facades is by Bernini.*

forms the counterpart of the Via della Lungara on the left bank. It was named after Giulius II who commissioned Bramante to build it, and is flanked by many palaces and churches. In the sixteenth century it was regarded as one of the most elegant Roman streets and today, too, though no longer leading through a quarter fashionable in the old sense, it maintains its distinction. Its most impressive ornaments are perhaps the hermae with their falcon heads displaying the family crest, which guard the facade of the Palazzo Falconieri. It was in the Via Giulia that Raphael had intended to build a palace for himself, but he died before his plans could be realized. Today there is not a single building left in Rome of which it could be said with certainty that it was inhabited by Raphael. In the long ancient Via dei Coronari, a narrow house of minor significance, is said to have belonged to him, and in his will he stipulated that the upkeep of his

THE PALAZZO
DI MONTECITORIO,
*begun by Bernini in 1650 and
finished by Carlo Fontana in 1690.*

tomb in the Pantheon should be paid for out of the rents. In the area of the old Campus Marcius too, is the only remaining building where it is certain that Michelangelo had resided, though only as a guest; this is the Palazzo Strozzi.

The Via del Governo Vecchio, today a narrow winding street in the old if not impoverished parts of the city, has a proud past. At a time when the Ponte Sant'Angelo provided the only direct link between the city and the Vatican, the Via del Governo Vecchio and some of its neighbouring streets provided the main access to the bridge and to the papal residence. It was a road of international significance and extremely fashionable. There were palaces, noble hostelries, houses of important merchants. This is the area where the banks developed, with those of Florence being preeminent. The names of the streets, Via dei Banchi Vecchi, Via dei Banchi Nuovi, Via del Banco

di Santo Spirito, still exist. The palazzo of the Bank of the Holy Spirit, the ancient treasury of the Curia, is still there and nearby the residence and bank of Agostino Chigi. There too, amidst the bankers, Benvenuto Cellini had his work-shop; he later moved to the Via Giulia, whence too, he had not far to go, as he frequently fell into disgrace, and was imprisoned in the Castel Sant'Angelo. The Via del Governo Vecchio was the route for the coronation processions of emperors, foreign ambassadors, processions of pilgrims and military parades. Here we find the Palazzo del Governo Vecchio, formerly a splendid cardinal's residence, containing plain offices today.

It is not difficult to imagine the one time importance of the streets leading up to the Ponte Sant'Angelo. In antiquity the Odeum of Domitian stood there, an imposing concert hall, as it might be decribed, from which derive the names of all the Odeons all over the world. In the centuries of decline, the debris came to form a hill on which the Orsini family, well known in medieval Rome, had settled. Mound and castle were called Monte Giordano after one of the favoured baptismal names of the Orsinis. Dante, in his Inferno, recalls the throng of pilgrims during the holy year, which, dividing into two streams, passed by this hill. The Palace as it is at present, with its Renaissance courtyard and a pretty Baroque fountain, has retained something of its old fortress character which defies the later peaceful accoutrements. It is not difficult to imagine oneself back in the time when the Orsinis, hereditary enemies of the Colonnas who were always loyal to the German Emperors, offered armed resistance to Henry VII on his way through and engaged in heavy street fighting with the Emperor whom

Dante celebrated as the bringer of peace. Henry had no choice but to have himself crowned in the Lateran instead of St Peter's.

Today the main approach to the Vatican is the Corso Vittorio Emanuele leading from the Piazza Venezia to the Tiber. Built a few years after the incorporation of Rome into the Italian kingdom, it cut through the maze of medieval houses, though with a reverence for some ancient buildings that was by no means characteristic of that time. The Corso as it were, politely makes way, wherever churches and palaces blocked its linear passage. How many great names of buildings there are! Half way along the Corso Vittorio Emanuele, adjoining the Campo dei Fiori, is the Palazzo della Cancelleria which contains the church of San Lorenzo in Damaso. The city of so many noble Renaissance palaces has none that is more magnificent than this palazzo with its gloriously columned courtyard, surely the most beautiful and harmonious one in Rome, though the artist who built it is not known. By some it is attributed to Bramante. The splendid structure of the facade clearly reflects the law of the golden section. As is often the case in Rome some of the Travertine stones to build it were taken from the Colosseum. In the courtyard antique granite columns were used, and the motifs of the facade recur on the third floor where the brick work has been covered by travertine, making a symmetrical and harmonious whole. Everything seems to fit in an unpretentious way and the onlooker himself feels he is included in the general harmony. Cardinal Riario who commissioned the palace had a rose in his crest which appears in the ornamentation of the facade, on each of the columns in the courtyard, even on the pavement in the centre where the drain for the rain water is shaped like a rose. There must be thousands of these rose motifs, but they do not bloom in the luxuriant freedom of nature nor as a super-natural symbol. It is a beautiful ornament of noble design and subject to a man-made symmetry.

Leaving the Cancelleria and walking eastwards one soon reaches the church of Sant'Andrea della Valle and further back the Gesù. The Piazza on which stands the principal church of the Jesuits in Rome is not particularly distinguished, but it leads on to a typical Italian feature. The Roman, and the Italian piazzas in general, as distinct from the squares of other cities, are not just widened streets or mere gaps between houses in a built-up area, but have a definite shape and purpose of their own. They often are like the stage in a theatre on which life is acted out passionately and colourfully. The players perform their allotted roles once and perhaps never again, but the day and the hour are always a link with eternity. The Gesù was built by Vignola and Giacomo della Porta who completed the Dome of St Peter's. This church opens up a new phase in sacred architecture, the Jesuit Baroque, which employed the full flood of artistic expression to the greater glory of God and his Saints. St Ignatius used it for his own purpose. Art plays with optical illusions; the incomplete dome is lined with dark material reversing its light-giving function, but the effect is amazing. If not making virtue out of necessity, it certainly produces a studied artfulness. Architecture is continued by means of painting, one merging into the other, painted pillars and columns thrusting into the painted heaven that decorates the ceiling. Two stars on the floor mark the spots where the optical illusion can be seen to its greatest effect. All of this may be just playfulness, and tricks of this kind may not be to everyone's liking. To be fair however, we should remember that the Baroque was the great age of the decorative art of the theatre, and indeed should remember the importance which the Jesuits attached to the theatre. Their cultural influence, after all, was rooted in Spain, the country of the great sacramental plays, the home of Calderon who embraced the whole of supernatural and natural life in the image of the world theatre. This Baroque delight in staging was intensified in Italy. Moreover, no flavour of condemnation as it exists in more puritanical climates attaches to the concept of the theatrical effects in the Baroque and Roman world. Wandering in the Gesù is like passing through a suite of marble palatial rooms or through the boxes and stalls of some court theatre. Given the Baroque premises, it is difficult to take exception to the result. The Piazza outside, one of the most beautiful in Rome, in a way continues the decorative and stage arts of the church interior. Perhaps no other piazza in the city is so unmistakably like a stage as this one. The subtle, delightful curve of the houses, seemingly forming a single front, creates the illusion of a closed half circle with only a part of the trapezoid-shaped building that faces the church jutting out. The streets opposite the church, leading away to the right and the left, are as little visible from its steps as are the stage entrances from the wings of a puppet theatre. Although there are five streets branching off the Piazza Sant'Ignazio you will not notice a single one when coming out of the church porch and standing between the two flanking pillars. The actors, as it were, make their appearances unnoticed. Suddenly they are on the stage, gesticulating, and equally suddenly, they disappear, having played their part. The church facade is of grey stone, the surrounding houses have that typical Roman colouring of somewhat pale brownish yellow; above them the blue Italian sky that also seems to have been provided by the producer. All these houses, their balconies decorated with flowers, appear to have the same height of four storeys, but this is an optical illusion created to harmonize exactly with the lower part of the church facade. Rising above it between pillars, and niches is the large single window which is really part of the upper structure with the open-work cross marking the gable.

I shall always remember the big mongrel that lay there one day, rather like a St Bernard, with white-yellow flecked long hair, curled up into a ball and nestling against the church porch in the sun. He was sleeping on an old greatcoat, the rope round his neck was tied to an iron door scraper. He was garding a bulging ruck-sack and two large cardboard boxes. Before him he had some brown wrapping paper with the remaining scraps of an ample meal. A black cat sneaked covetously closer, but every time she came within jumping distance, fear restrained her and she drew back. It was a pantomime which, I imagined, could have been set to music. No human being was in sight. The owner of the dog, ruck-sack and cardboard boxes, might have been saying his prayers inside the church or he might have had some business to attend to in the neighbourhood. Perhaps he was playing his part on another piazza!

The Piazza della Minerva, south-west of Sant' Ignazio, derives its unified character from the front of the Dominican church and the delightful elephant obelisk, designed by Bernini, which dominates it. How patiently, but also how lightly this elephant seems to carry the burden of his obelisk. Its head turned to the right, the trunk curled up and back, the front legs somewhat close together, the face and look expressive, human, yet without losing its animal features – how very different from the ordinary elephant sculptures of earlier ages. Over the animal's back hangs a long saddlecloth decorated with tassles and the Chigi coat of arms, for it was Pope Alexander VII of the Chigi family who had the monument erected and dedicated to divine wisdom, and it was he who supplied the inscription. It states that strength should carry wisdom, as the elephant being the strongest animal bears the obelisk, that is decorated with Egyptian wisdom emblems and points to the sky. But at the same time the elephant embodies also wisdom itself, as the ancient peoples had always believed, and wisdom in its turn suggests Minerva, the original patron of the place. The Dominicans from Florence built this church over the ruins of the Domitian Temple of Minerva and by so doing introduced the Gothic style to Rome. The many rose shaped and stained glass windows and the colourful twilight of the interior intensify the Gothic effect of the architectural forms, although, of course, it is not a Gothic style with which people of northern Europe are familiar. For them it may seem like hearing a song familiar from childhood but sung in a strange tongue, though they will recognize it by the tune.

Between the Piazza Navona and the Piazza del Governo Vecchio, is the church of Santa Maria dell'Anima built in the sixteenth century and used by the Germans and Dutch in Rome. It contains the fine tomb of Hadrian VI, who died in 1523; he was formerly tutor and then counsellor to the Emperor Charles V, the last non-Italian pope. Next door is the church of Santa Maria della Pace, the magnificent cloister of which was designed by Bramante, and bears comparison with the famous Tempietto with which Bramante first introduced his great art to Rome. The subtle and gentle effect of this place reveals a temperament in which all spiritual forces and currents are harmonized with each other in perfect proportion. There is a beautiful still vitality about it without in the least damaging the symmetry of the pillars in the upper storey which rise over the arches of the lower arcades. Such harmony is a tremendous sensual experience. Nowadays apartments surround the little cloister and one envies those living there, able to look out every morning on the dome of Our Lady of Peace. The church itself below the dome forms an octagon from which a short nave protrudes. Particularly fine is the semi-circular pillared portico, added to the facade in the middle of the seventeenth century by Pietro da Cortona. Even for Rome this is a rare architectural experience, and how well it fits into the street pattern!

Above the altar there is a splendid fresco of the Virgin Mary with St Catherine and St Brigida as the Italians call St Bridget, known as Brigitta in her own country, Sweden. She lived in Rome for twenty years, first in a house on the later Piazza Farnese where a small church was built in her honour, and then in Via Panisperna, near San Lorenzo. Like St Catherine of Siena who lies under the high altar of Santa Maria Sopra Minerva, St Bridget was active in exerting her power and influence to bring the popes back from their exile in Avignon.

It is not, however, the frescoes by Baldassare Peruzzi to which Santa Maria della Pace owes its fame, but the fresco of the four sibyls which, commissioned by Agostino Chigi, Raphael painted over the arcade of the first chapel on the right. This is a work of warm humanity, grace, and sweet movement. It is as though Raphael, dominated as he often felt by the presence of Michelangelo, had never set foot into the Sistine Chapel; here he seems completely independent and himself. His sibyls are not powers of fate, they are sisters of man and like man, subject to the fates which they have to record and proclaim.

This part of the city, where it protrudes farthest to the west, is like a peninsula surrounded by the bending river. It is the district of narrow medieval streets and Baroque churches, and it is also connected with the strange figure, so characteristic of sixteenth-century Rome, of San Filippo Neri, "the saint with a sense of humour" as he has been called. He was not born in Rome, but like so many others he became a Roman, indeed an apostle of Rome. He worked among the people and became famous for his appeal to individual souls. A chapel built in the Palazzo Massimi on the Corso Vittorio Emanuele recalls an incident in which he saved the life of a child. Various memories of his personal life and radiating influence are preserved in Roman churches, such as in San Giovanni dei Fiorentini, the church of his compatriots in the Via Giulia where he worked for ten years, and in San Girolamo della Carità near the Palazzo Farnese, where altogether he spent thirty-two years. Also linked with him are the Catacombs of San Sebastiano, the only catacomb site which had survived the Middle Ages, which he loved to visit in the evening to pray there, as did St Bridget two centuries before him. He is most vividly brought to life, however, in the Chiesa Nuova, the New Church, on the Corso Vittorio Emanuele and in the palace adjoining it, built by Borromini, backing on to the house and hostel of the Oratorian Fathers in the Via del Governo Vecchio, with its oratory, a big hall used for religious lectures and concerts. This is the place whence the musical term "oratory" has entered our language. On the left of the high altar is the Saint's burial chapel. His body can be seen lying under the altar, the face covered with a silver mask modelled on his death mask. Above it a copy of the famous portrait by Guido Reni shows the expressive features of his bearded face, the Saint kneeling in his chasuble before an apparition of the Virgin Mary surrounded by angels. At the entrance to the chapel stands the simple pulpit from which, in a sitting position, he used to preach. The Oratorian Fathers still use it today; the more imposing pulpit in the church is used by guest preachers. The atmosphere surrounding this saint exudes heart-warming simplicity and this is particularly felt in the rooms where he lived.

A small chapel upstairs in the house of the Fathers of the Oratory contains many relics, poems and letters in his hand-writing, his bed, and that most uncomfortable looking structure, the confessional in which he used to spend up to seven hours at a time, so as not to disappoint anyone of the innumerable people who came for advice and consolation. Between the bed and the confessional stands an altar with the original painting by Guido Reni. The room in which he died has been moved, walls, floor and ceiling, into the room adjoining the chapel. It contains the altar where he celebrated Mass. Often he was so carried away by devotion and ecstasy that his Mass sometimes lasted two hours, by which time the altar servers had permission to leave.

Filippo Neri was a close friend of St Charles Borromeo and the great church historian Baronius, and both had frequently to intervene when their friend was in trouble with the ecclesiastical authorities, which happened quite frequently, since a man of his natural simplicity and originality had difficulty in conforming to the official clerical pattern. Part of his originality was the unconcerned way in which he introduced new features such as allowing lay-people and children to preach, and getting women and choirs to sing the responses in church. In his day this could not fail to shock the traditionalists. His love for young people and children has been kept alive in the community which he founded. Filippo Neri liked to mix with the Roman youth. He used to play with them and to teach them at the same time under the old oak tree linked with the name of the poet Torquato Tasso, behind Sant'Onofrio, or at the Villa Celimontana on the Coelian Hill. There under ever-green oak trees, looking out over gardens and the Campagna towards the hills, he sat at the feet of an ancient sarcophagus and, as the inscription says, talked with his disciples of divine things.

He also initiated the Oratorian pilgrimage of the Sette Chiese in which, on the third Sunday after Easter, thousands of people take part to this day, singing the old Oratorian hymn of the Vanità di Vanità, vanity of vanities, all of sixteen verses. The pilgrimage begins at the Chiesa Nuova, proceeds to St Peter and St Paul, branching off at the Via delle Sette Chiese shortly before reaching the Basilica of San Paolo; it then moves up hill, passing another Oratorian chapel, across the old catacomb area and reaching San Sebastiano after about three quarters of an hour. The way back leads along the Via Appia to the city, with a break for lunch at the Villa Celimontana; the procession then passes on to San Giovanni in Laterano, the church of the Holy Cross and to Santa Maria Maggiore, ending where it began at the Chiesa Nuova.

This is the traditional Roman pilgrims' way, that centuries ago was familiar to the devout from all over the world. It takes in the greater part of the city omitting only those areas which, at the time when the pilgrimage originated were not as yet part of the city area and possessed no churches of importance. The route alone is therefore evidence of the distant origin of the pilgrimage in which the seven main churches of Rome have, as it where, replaced the seven Kings and the seven hills, thus manifesting, that the city which alone is called eternal, had entered a new age.

LEAVING ROME

Saying fairwell to Rome is painful and heartbreaking. It brings home to one the insufficiency of human existence. Those who depart, be it after a short visit or after years, depart with the consciousness of hardly having begun and no one knows whether he can be certain of returning.

It is an old custom before leaving to drink from the Fontana di Trevi and to throw a coin into its waters. Whoever does so, it is said, assures his return. But for the less savoury drinking part it is a laudatory custom well worth following. But anyhow, if one can spend only a few days in Rome one need not worry, for even if one had twenty or forty years to live there one would not be able to exhaust what the city has to offer. If a man had the capacity to live in Rome for a century or two and in full possession of his faculties, he might be entitled to claim that he had drained the cup. But mankind is meant to drink from thimbles, and in Rome a thimble more or less would make no difference. Acquisition of knowledge ought not to be the purpose of a visit to Rome, for knowledge is quickly forgotten and remains fragmentary. One goes to Rome to experience a deepening of the spirit, and this is something that can never be lost. Those who come only for a few days may indeed be more fortunate, for they will retain the image of Rome with all the force of first impressions. With luck they will avoid the discovery that in Rome no less than elsewhere one is afflicted by all the troubles, small and large, of the corruptible human condition. Man is not made to remain in a euphoric state for ever, like the bird of Paradise in the fairy tale who had no feet and was thus saved from the contaminating touch of the earth. It is better to leave Rome with that everlasting longing which is more than fulfilment, with a kind of homesickness as an image of man's desire for an eternal home.

To have spent some time in Rome, however little, is indeed to have lived through ages and centuries. One adds a new dimension to one's experience in life that makes all those daily, petty, human concerns seem very shallow indeed. One's vision is constantly taken up with objects of significance or at least with delightful things. And that surely sharpens the senses. One tends to judge experiences, encounters, whether with other men, with fate, works of art, ideas, landscapes or places, according to the extent of their transforming power. In Rome one is in the city of supreme universality which radiates into time and space. The visitor will experience that mysterious capacity of Rome to absorb new features, from the obelisks of Egypt onwards, and to fuse them into a living pattern with what is old. He will be over-

THE VILLA D'ESTE
*in Tivoli, 30 miles outside Rome in
the Campagna, built in 1550,
is famous for its beautiful gardens.*

whelmed by a great sense of permanence, of natural continuity which even volcanic upheavals do no more than disturb, but never destroy; indeed, he will be overwhelmed by what one may almost call finite eternity. To have been in Rome is to have received an extension of the limits of human finiteness. It is like surveying, by way of extracts and in one single place, the destiny of the world, as though sitting in, if only as an observer, at the counsel of the gods. The ancients used to say of the Zeus of Otricoli, that he who had seen his face would never again be unhappy. I am inclined to think that he who is fortunate enough to have stayed in Rome would be unable to go on living as though nothing had happened. In Rome, more than anywhere else, we feel that there is something of the pilgrim in each one of us. One would wish that the promise of that homecoming could be felt by each pilgrim.

INDEX OF ILLUSTRATIONS

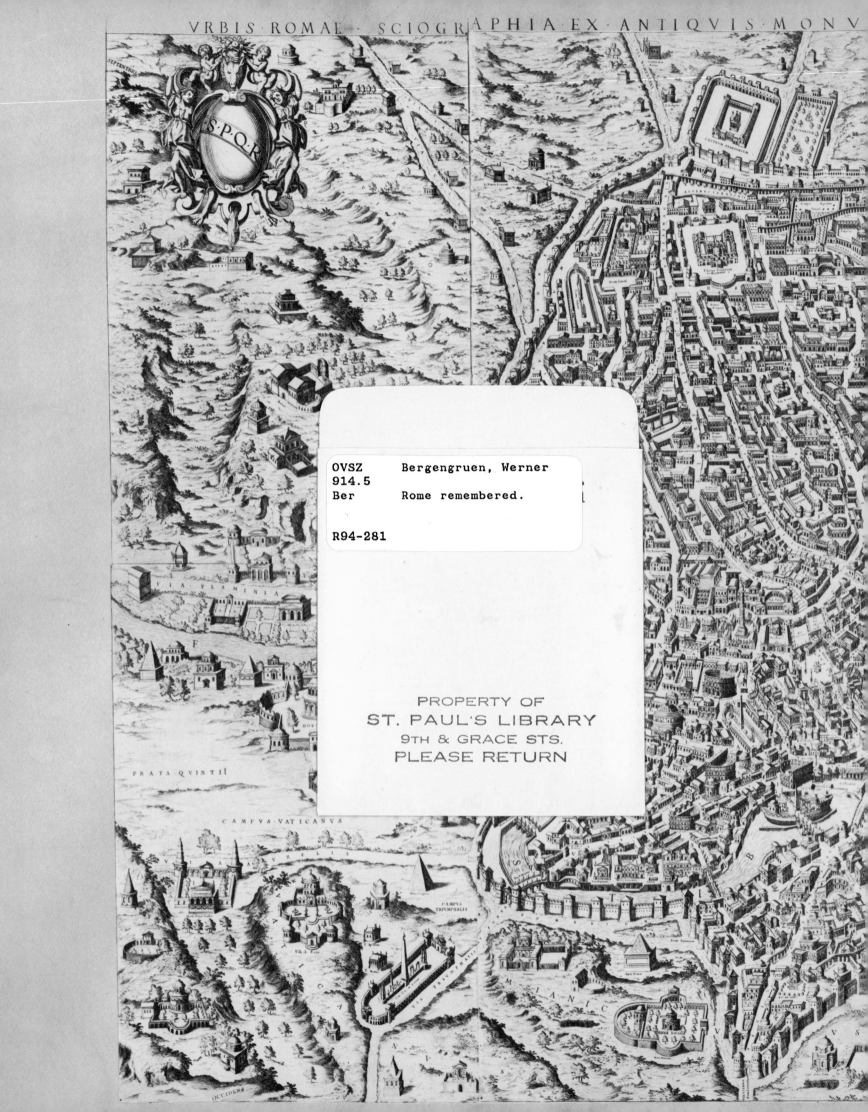